AF425264

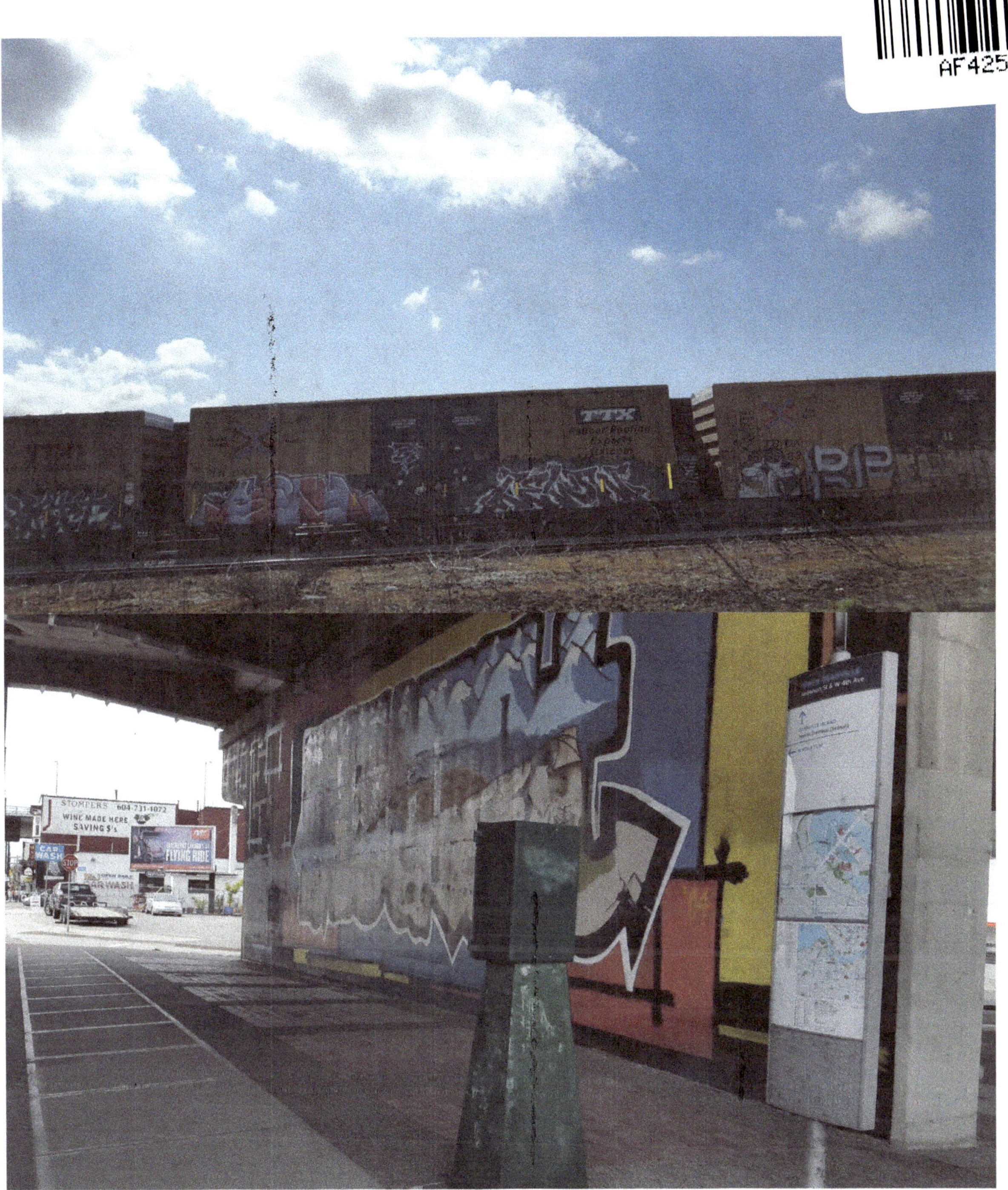

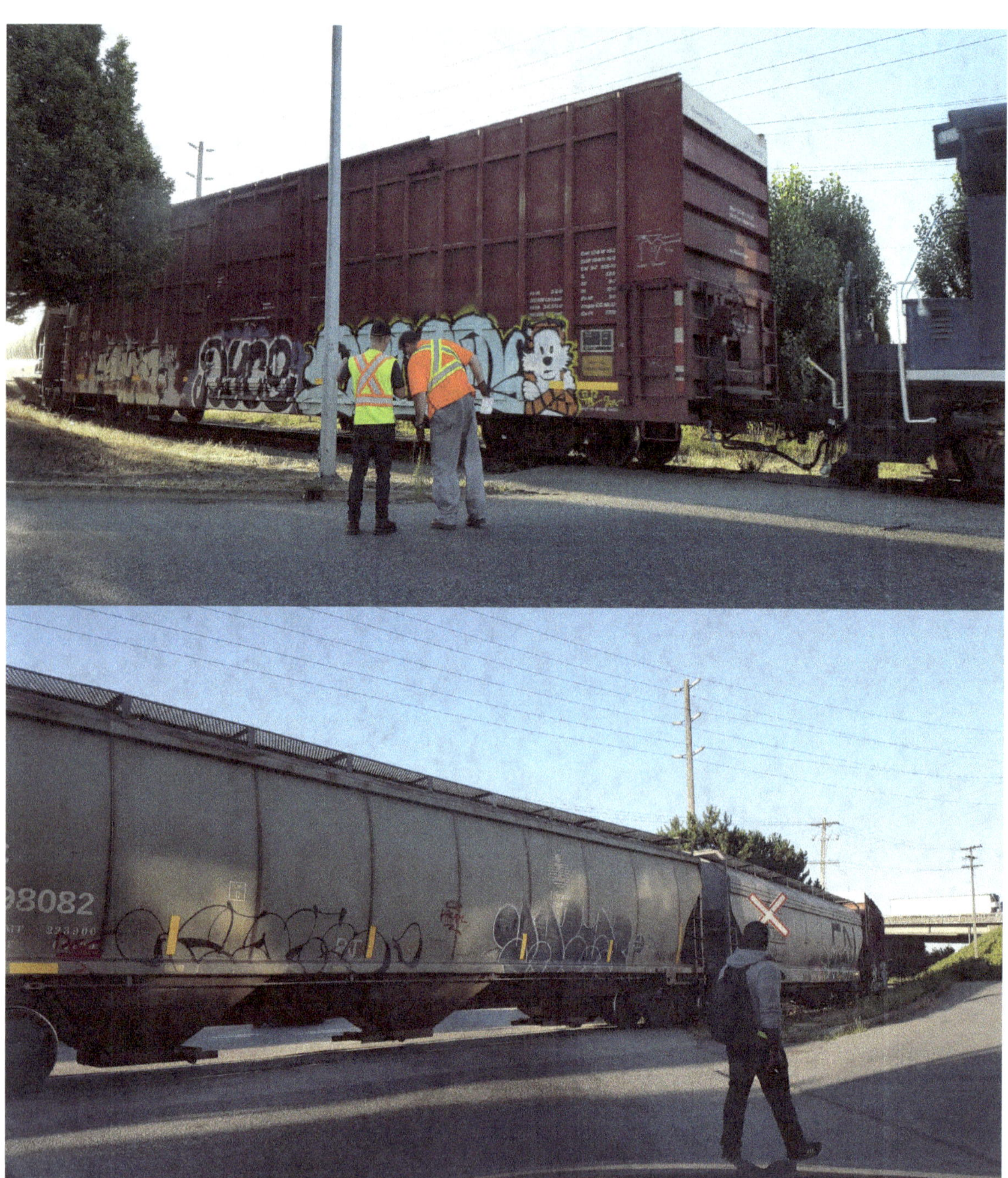

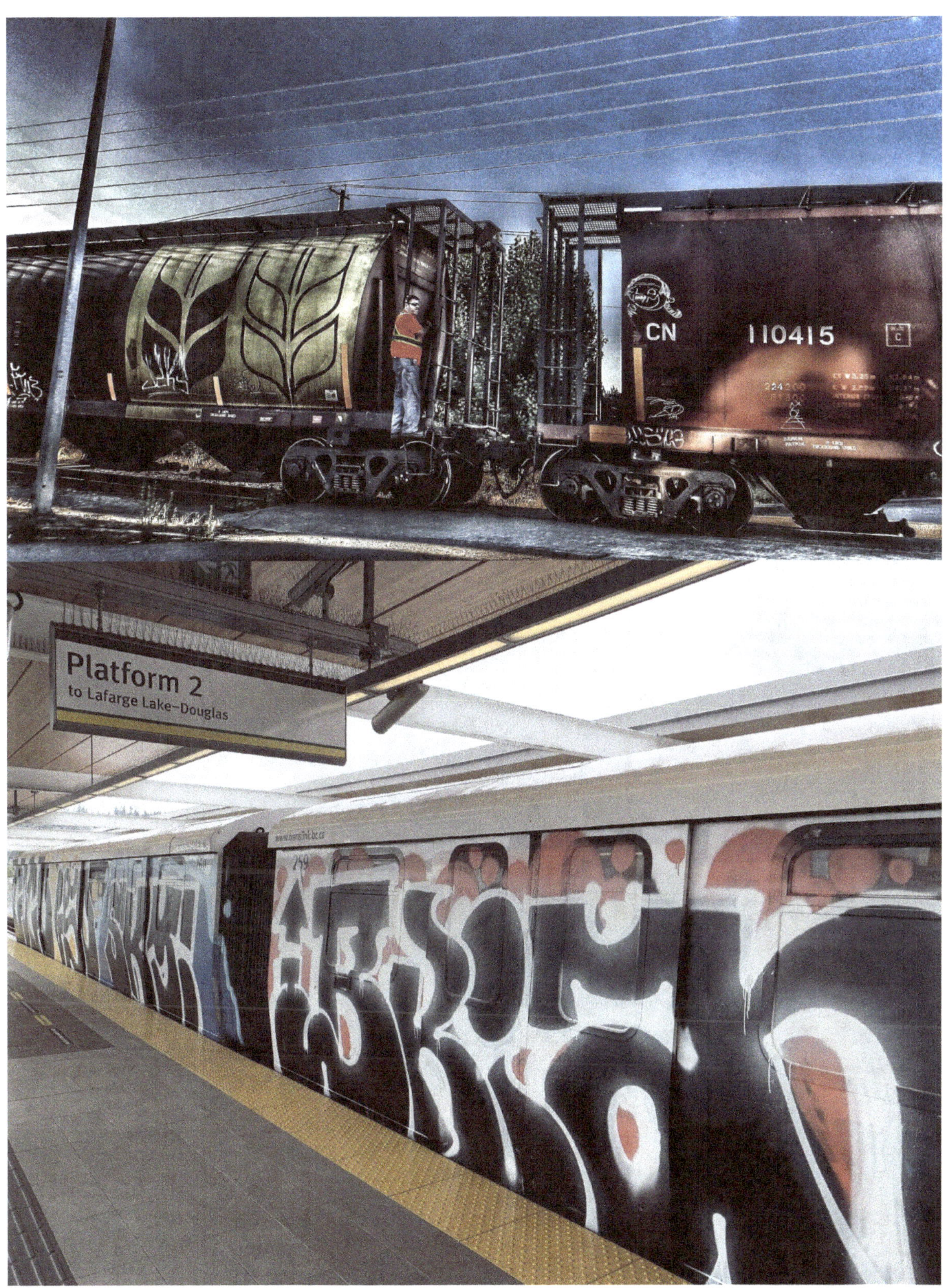
CN
110415
Platform 2
to Lafarge Lake–Douglas

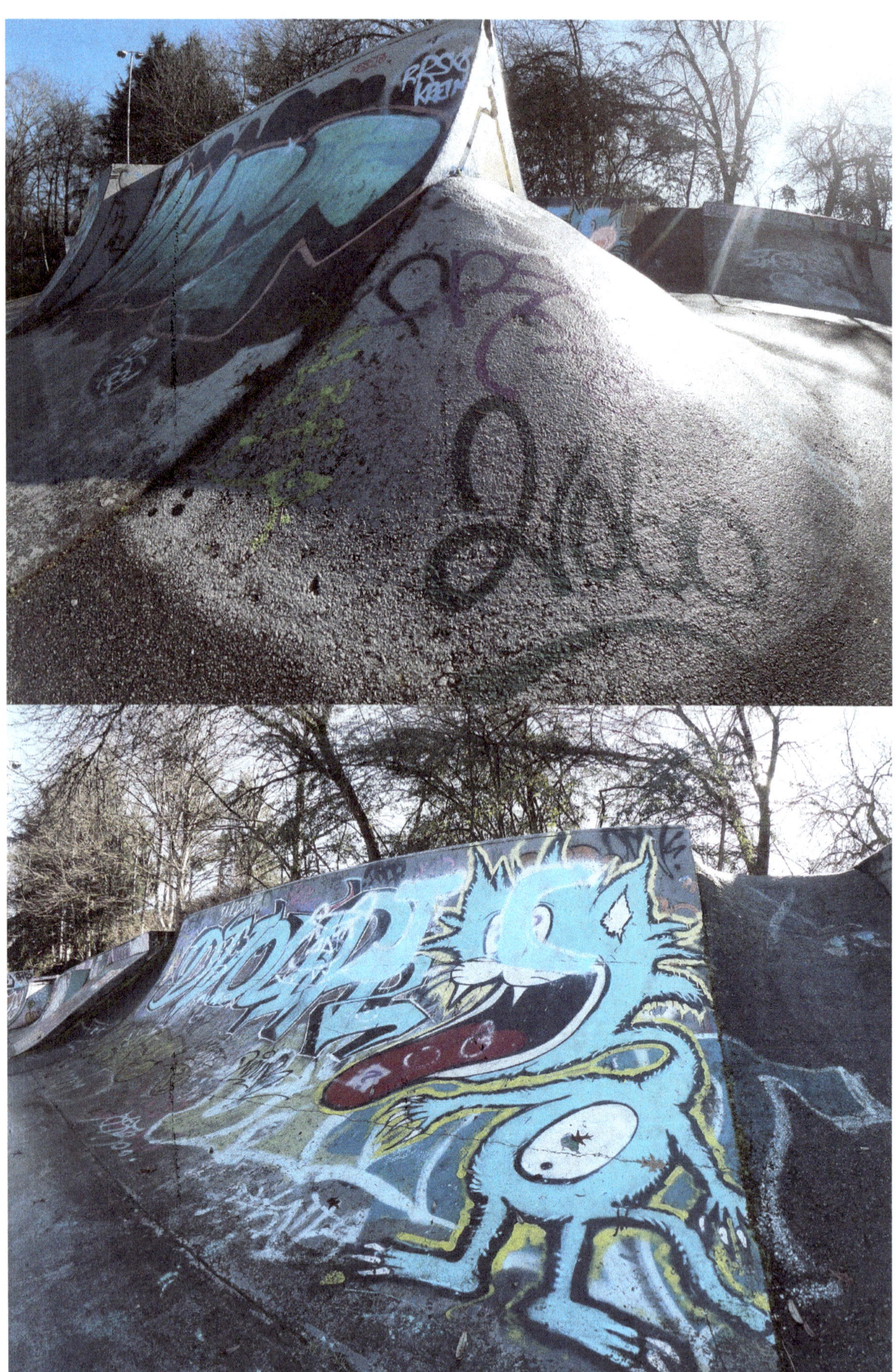

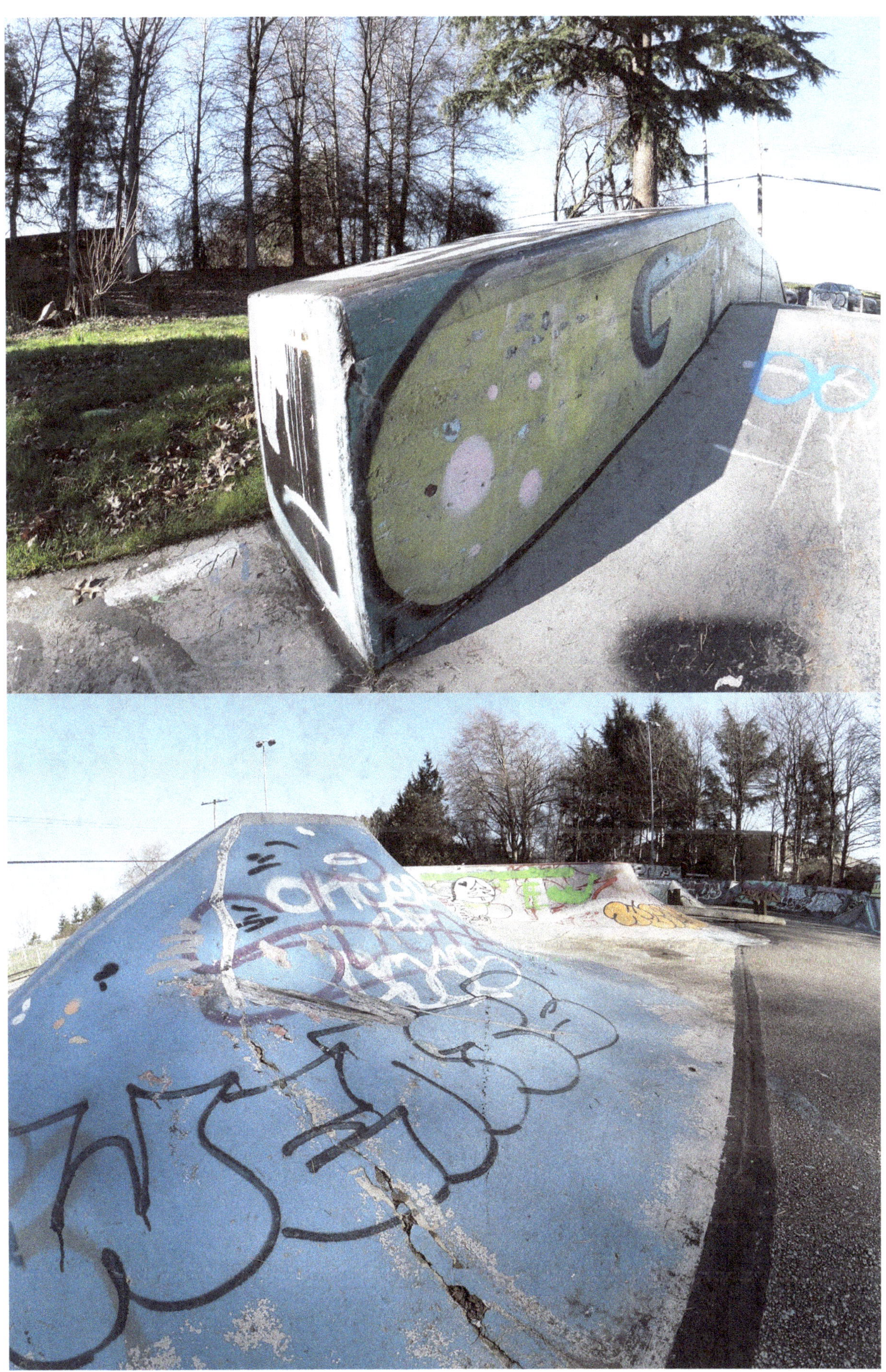

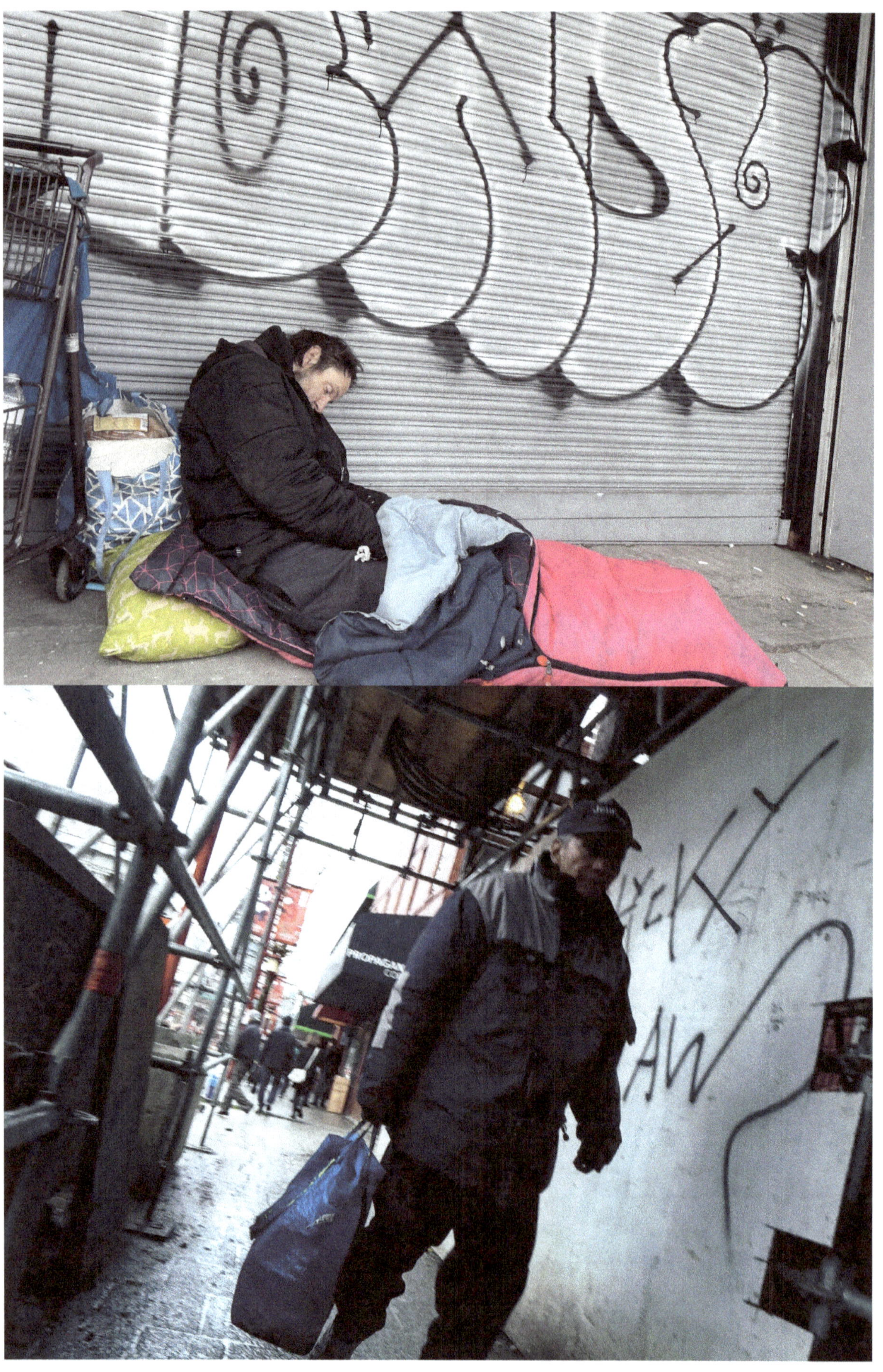

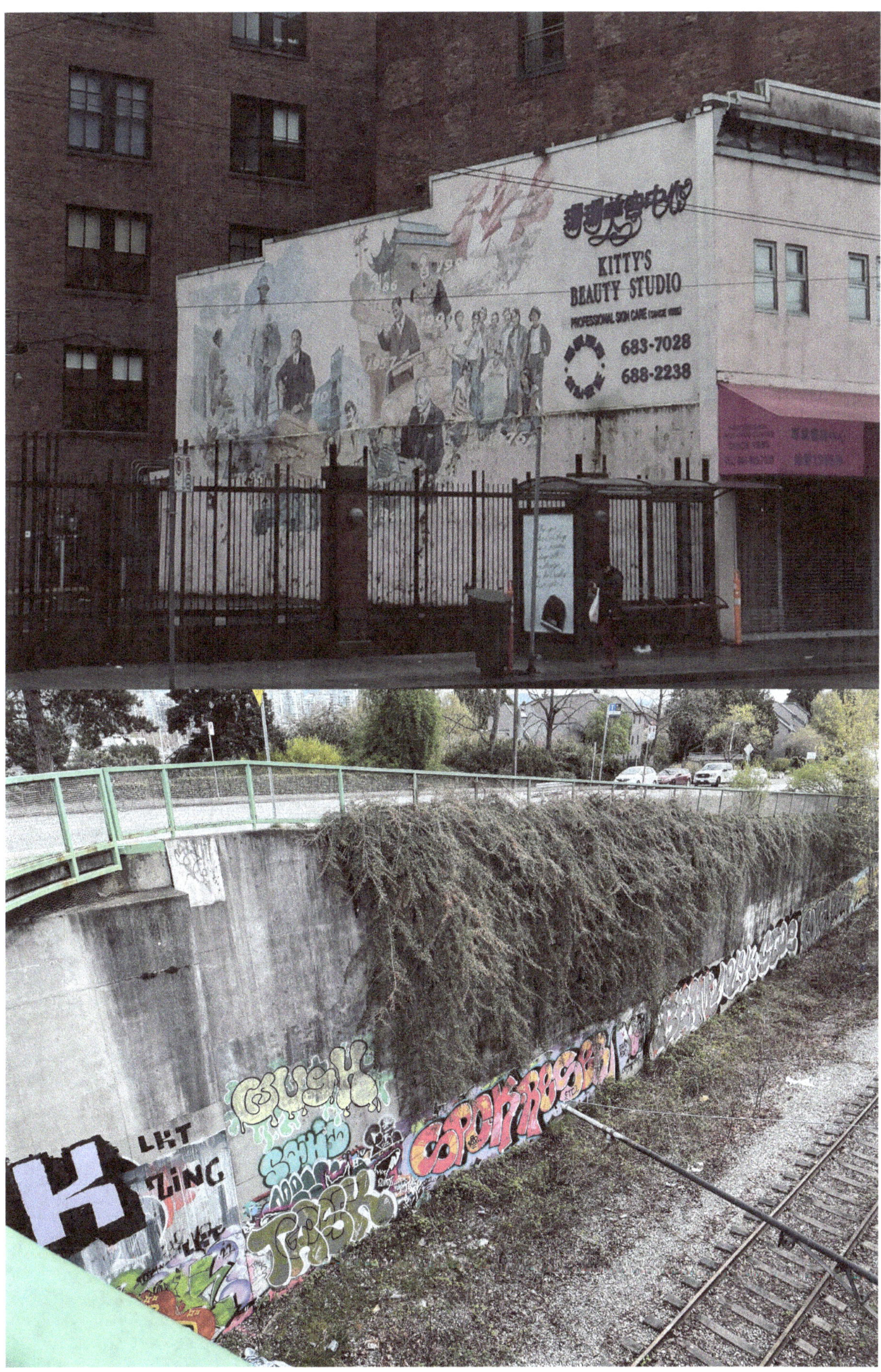

KITTY'S
BEAUTY STUDIO
PROFESSIONAL SKIN CARE (SINCE 1982)
683-7028
688-2238

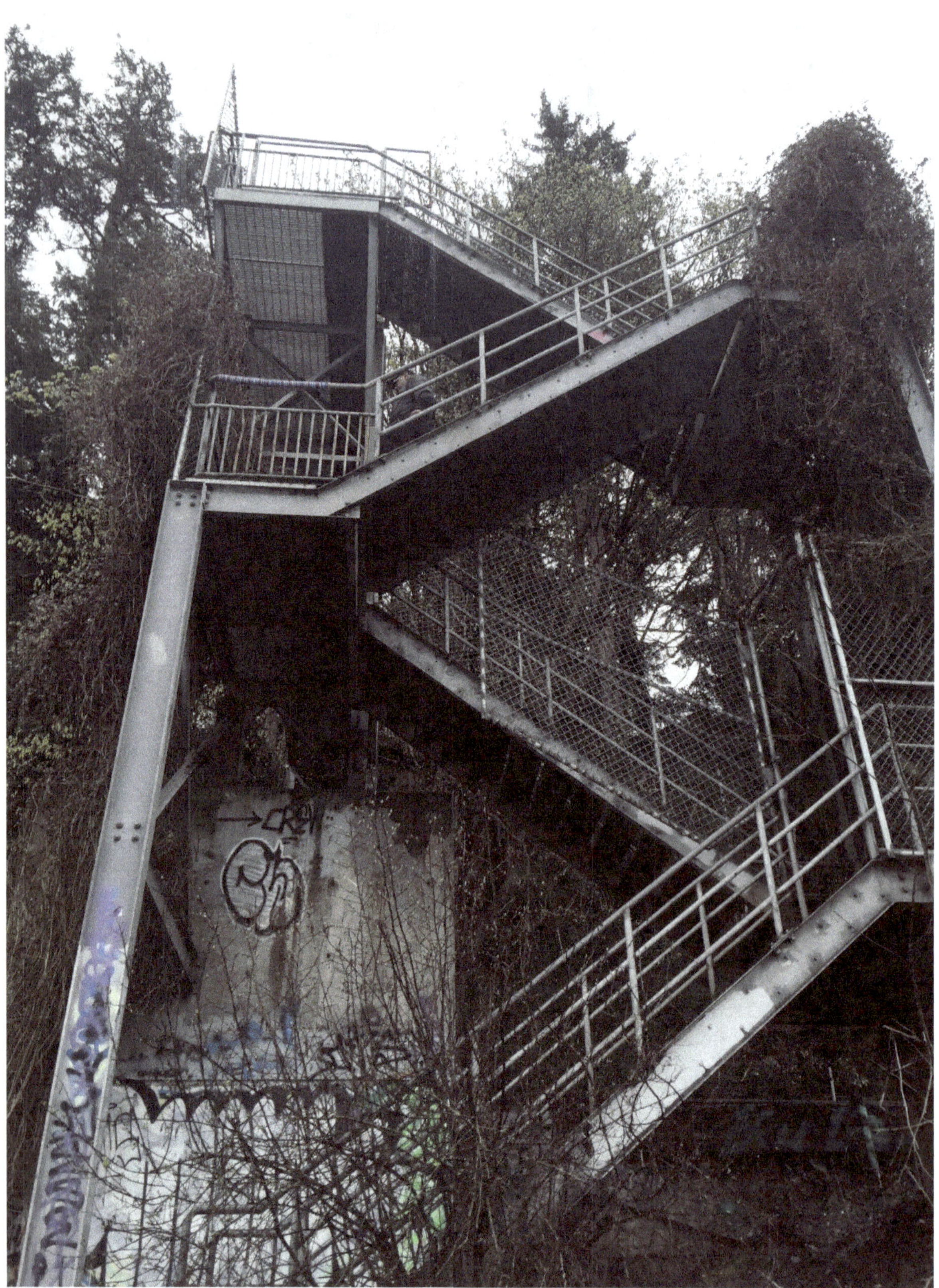

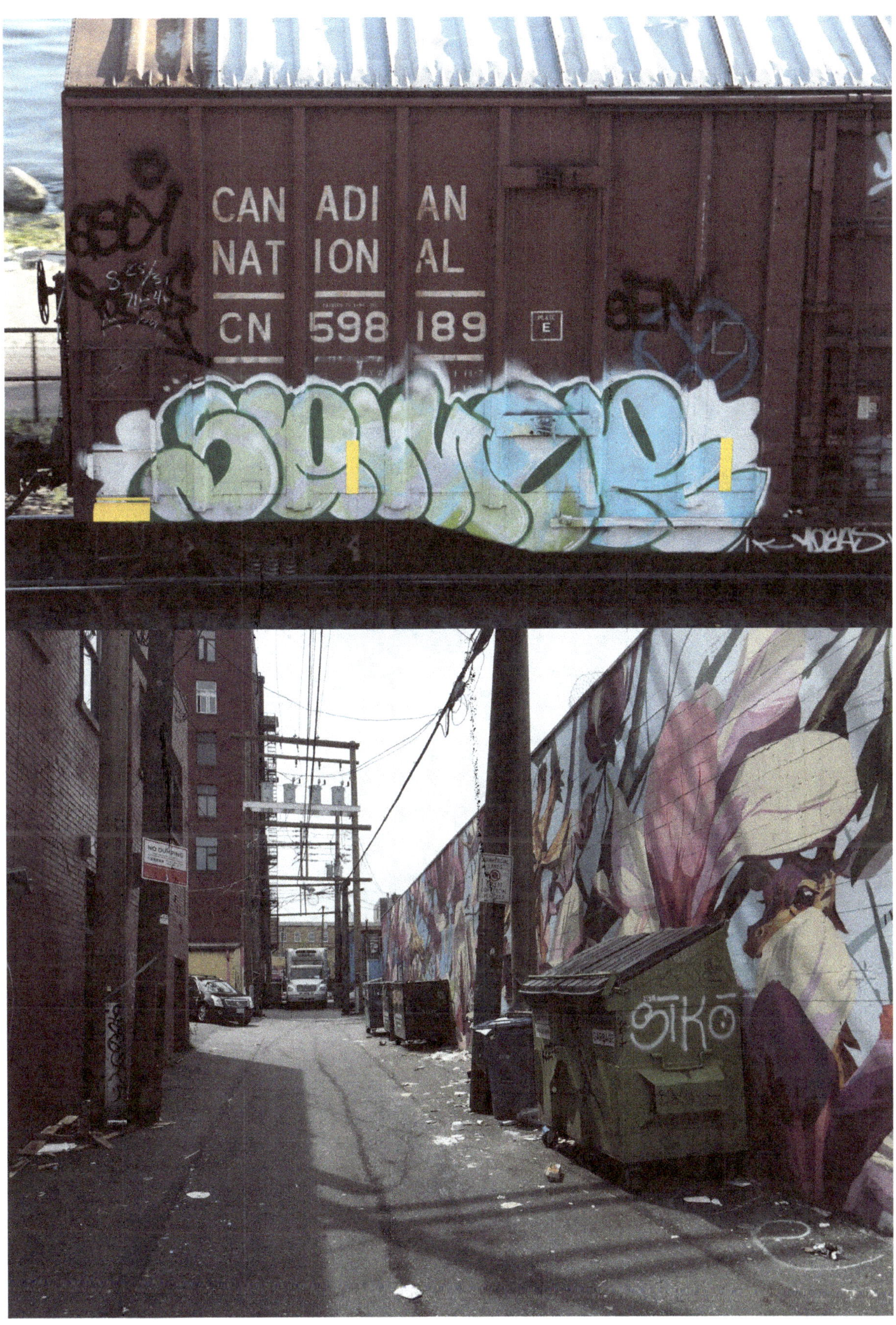

CAN ADI AN
NAT ION AL
CN 598 189
PLATE
E

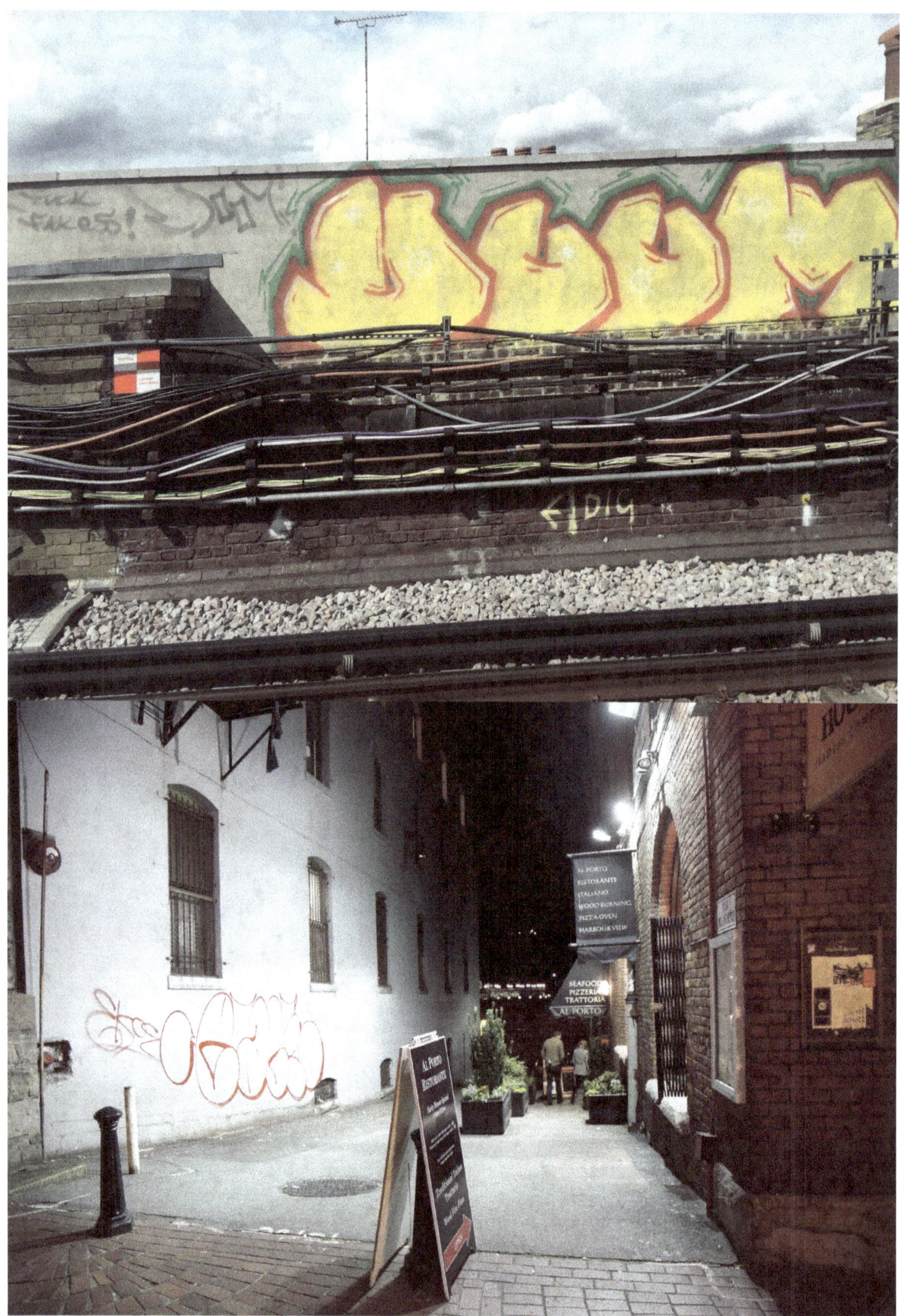

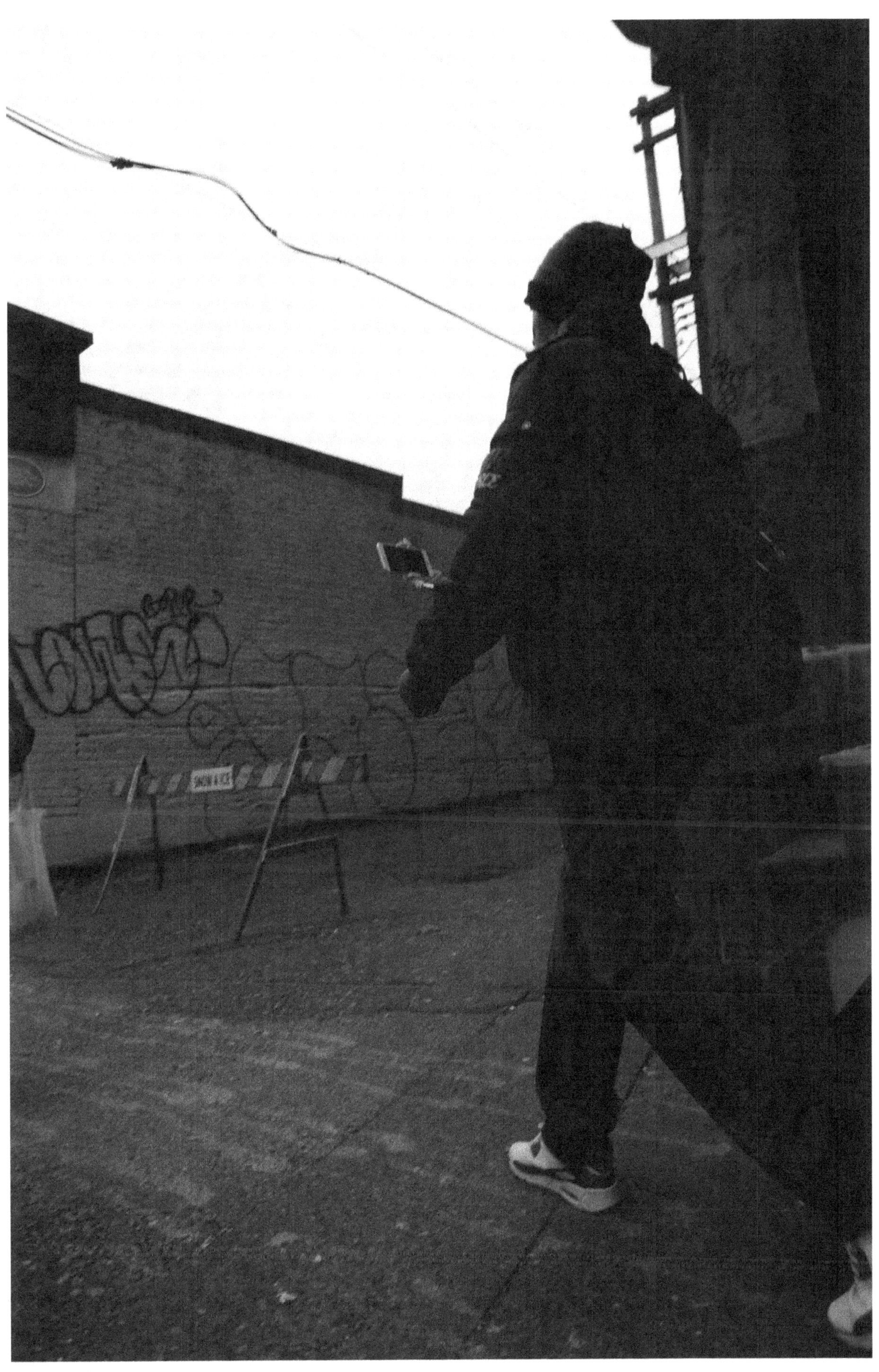

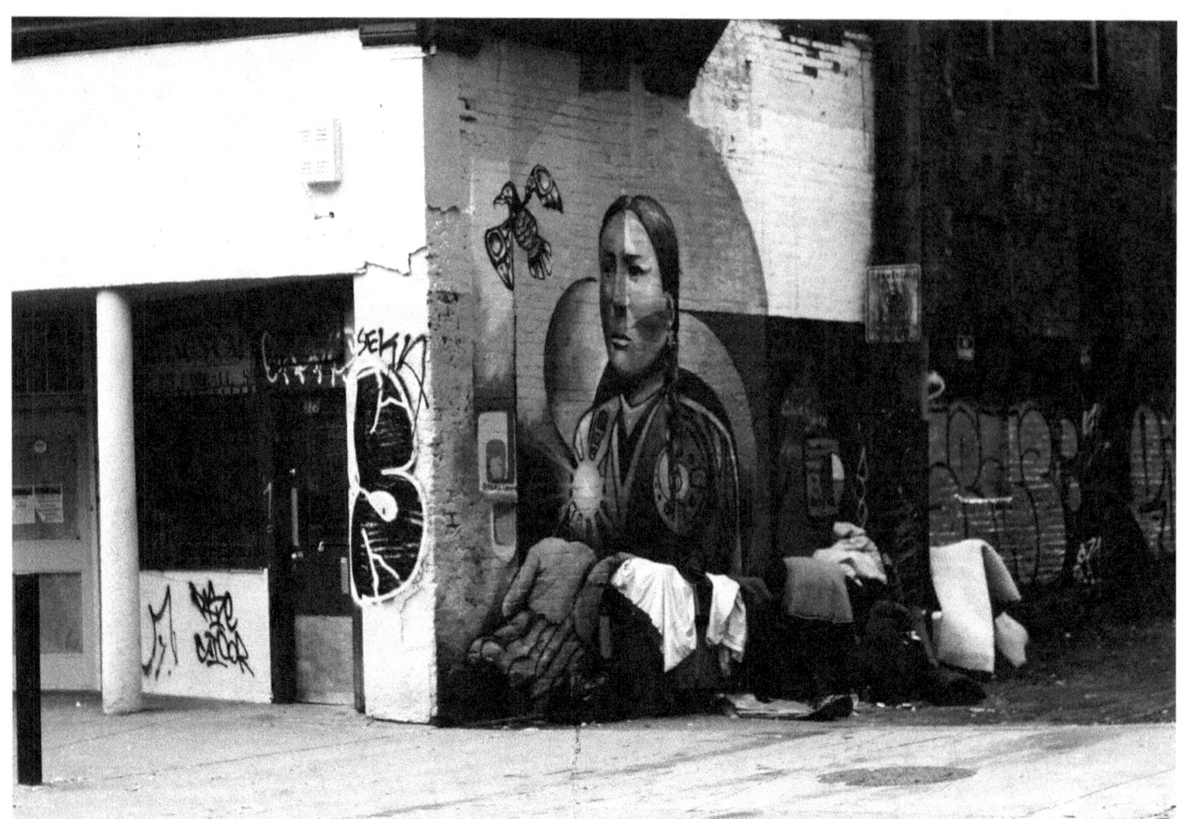

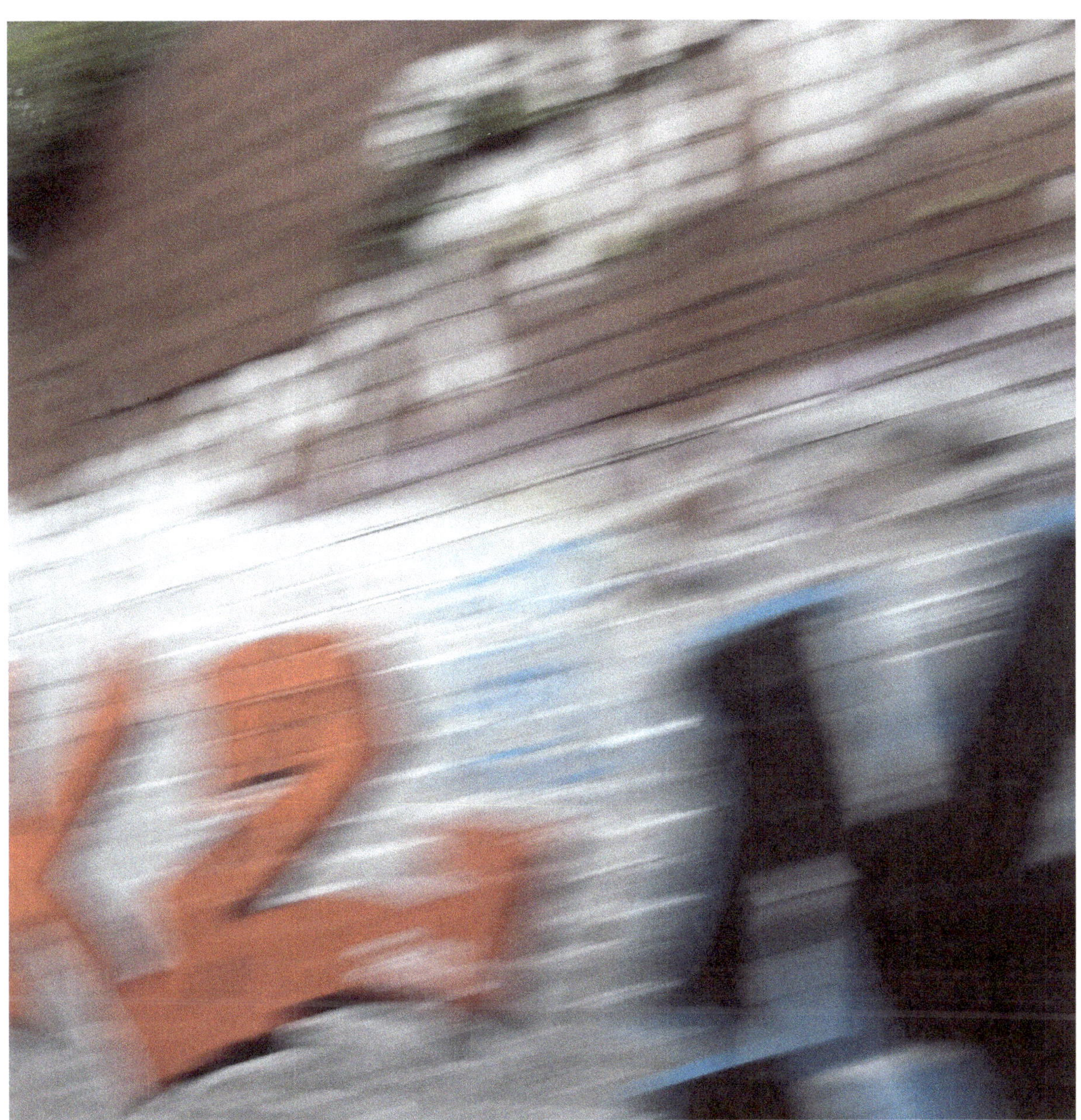

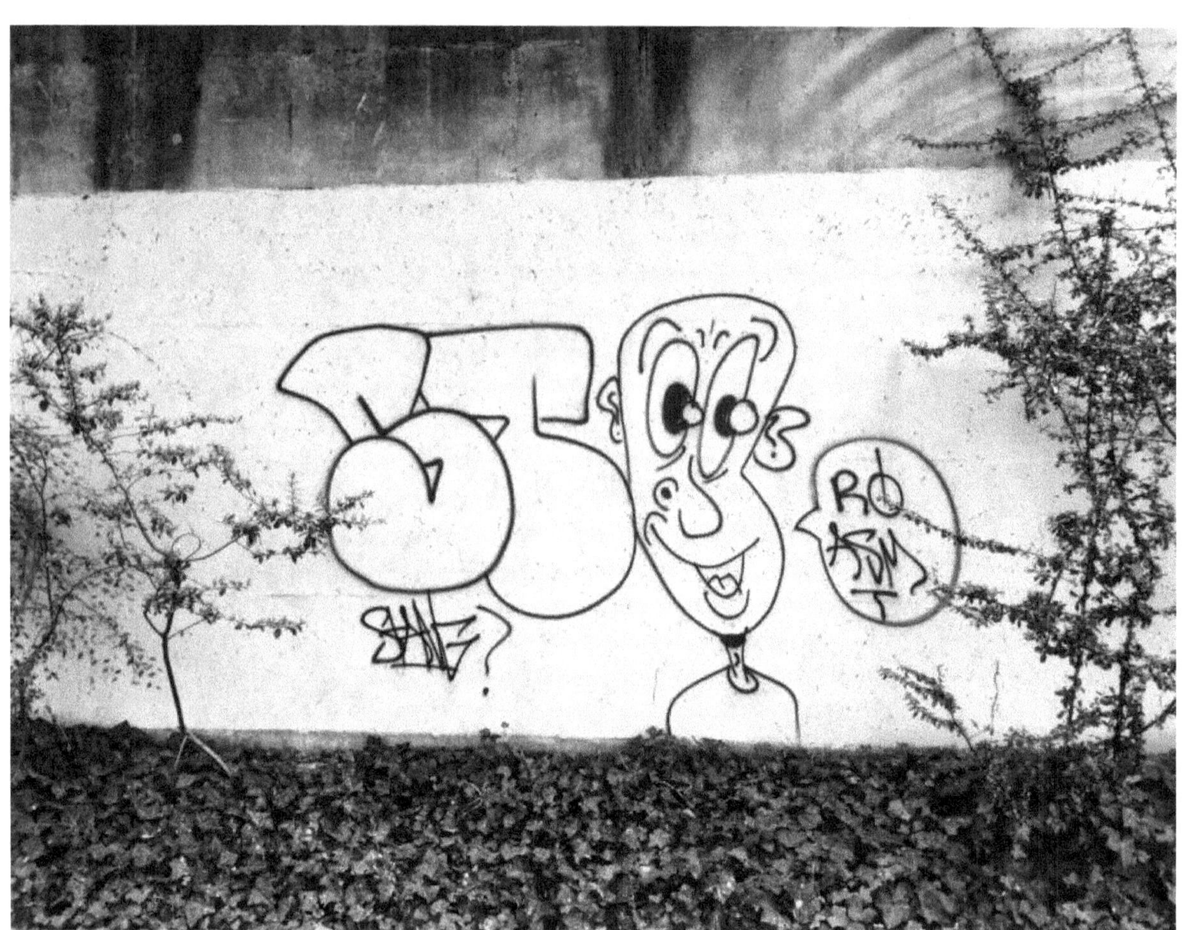

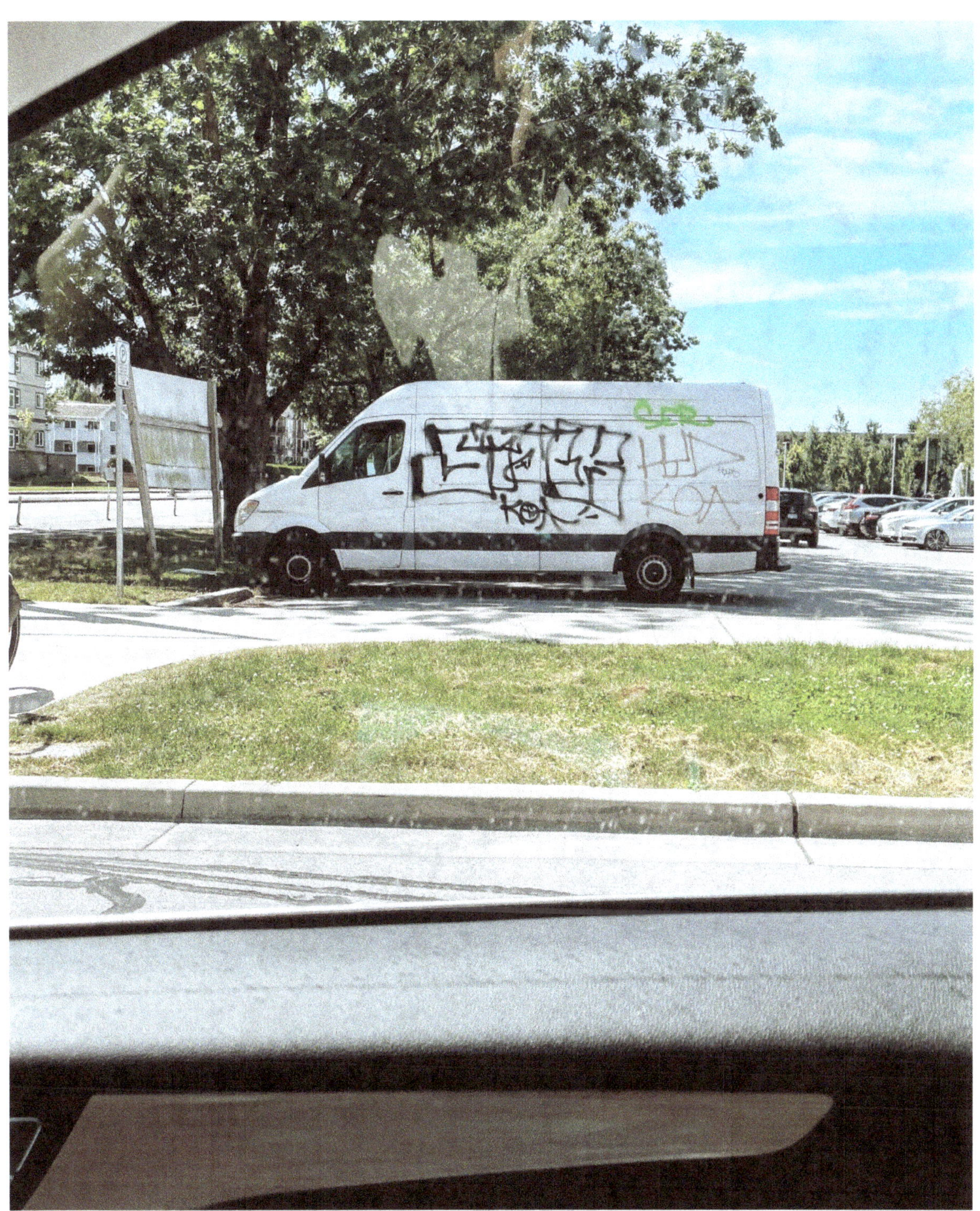

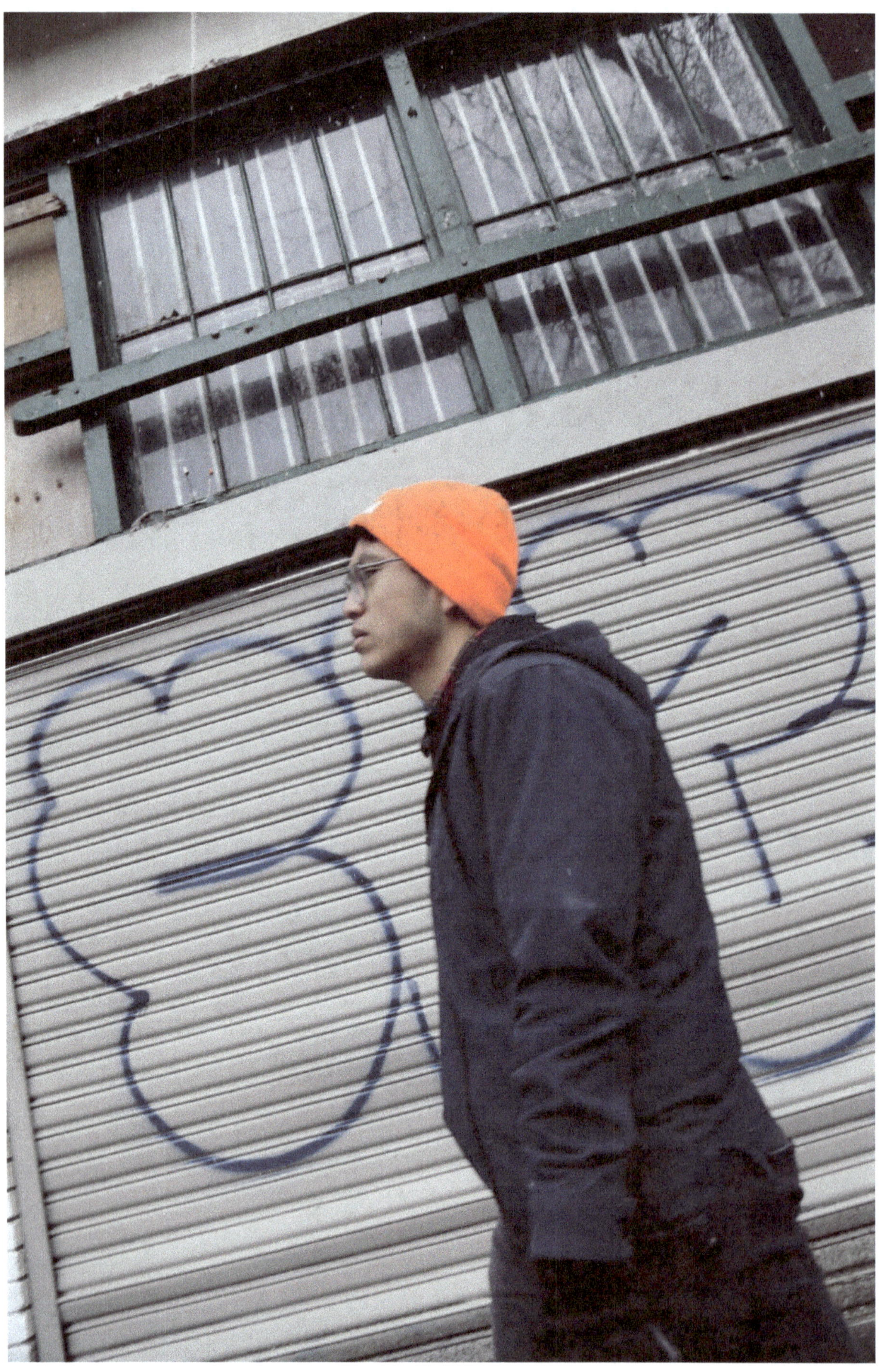

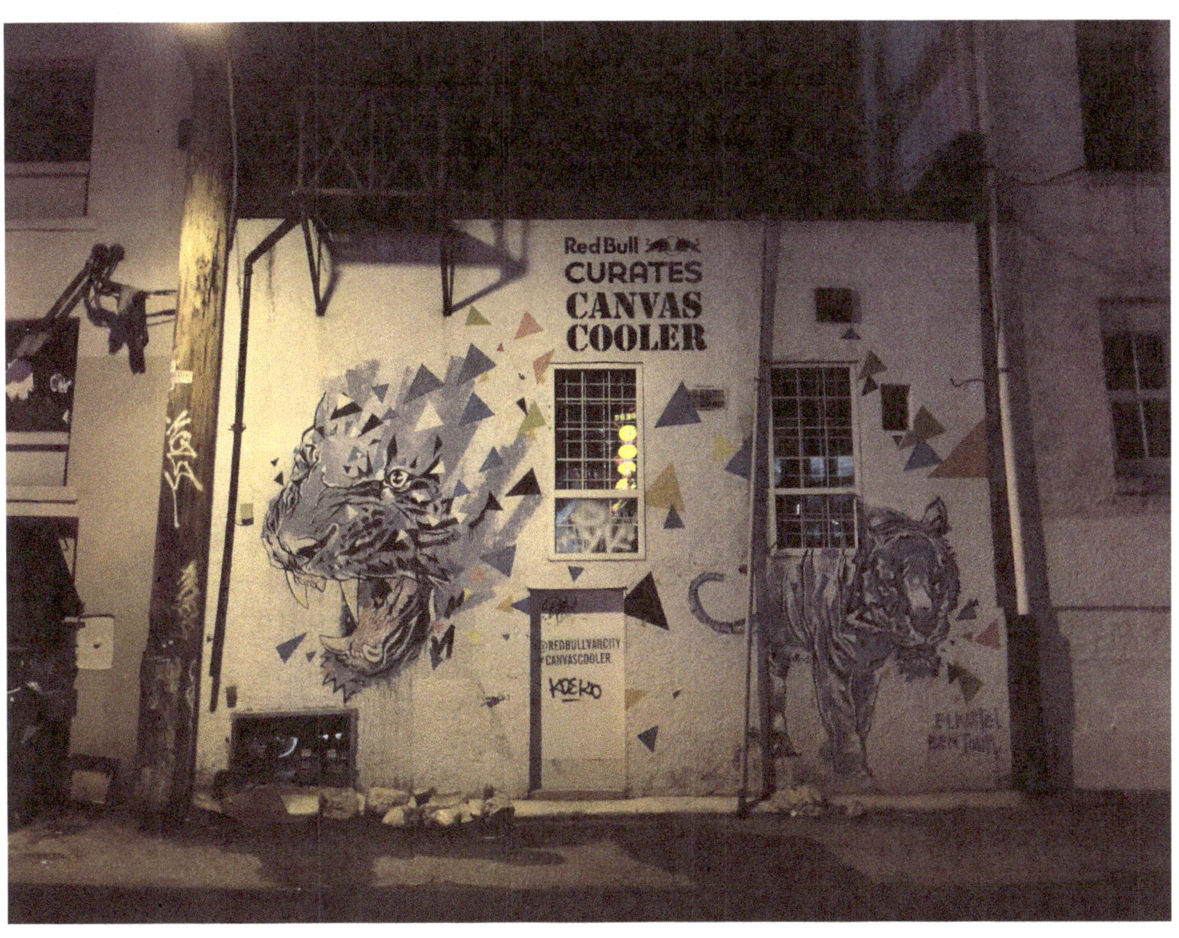

RedBull
CURATES
CANVAS
COOLER
@REDBULLVANCITY
#CANVASCOOLER

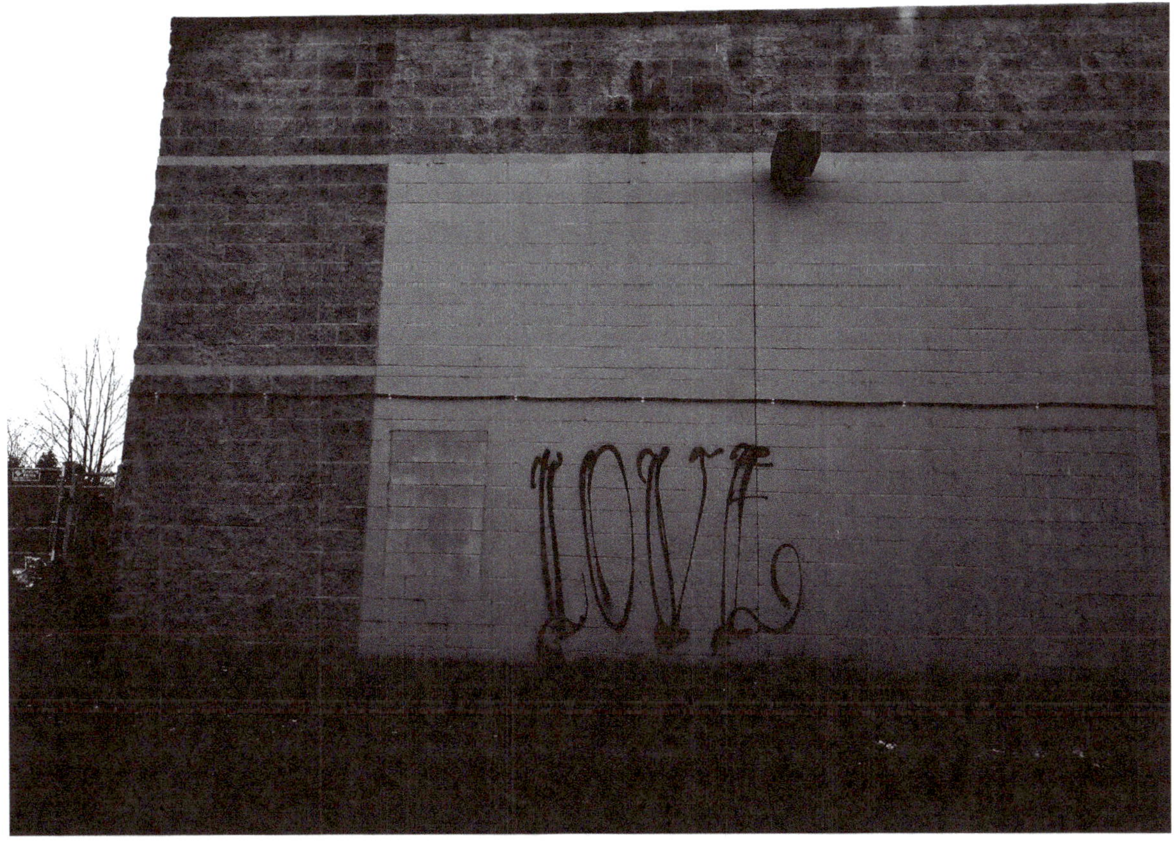

LOVE

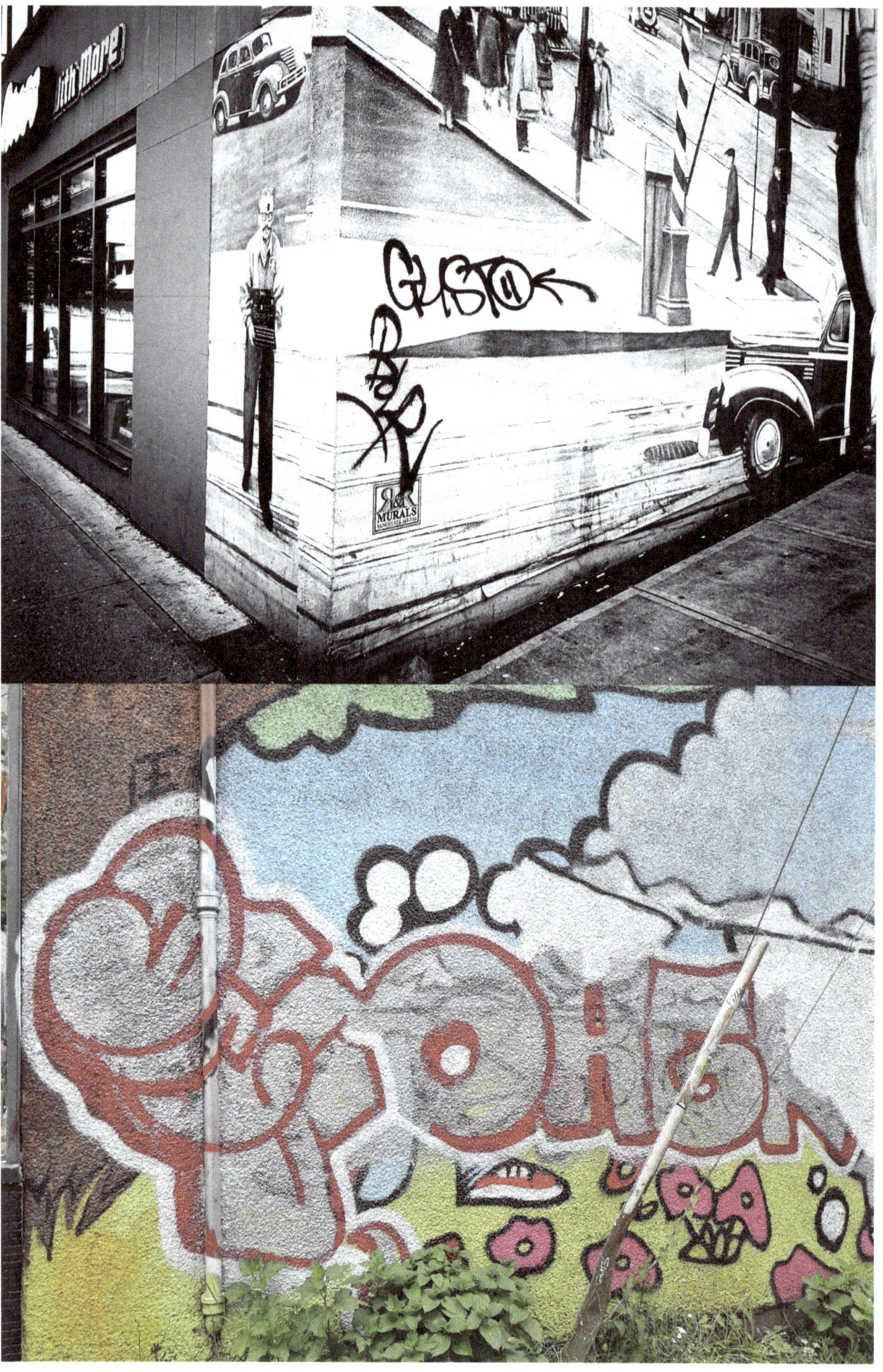

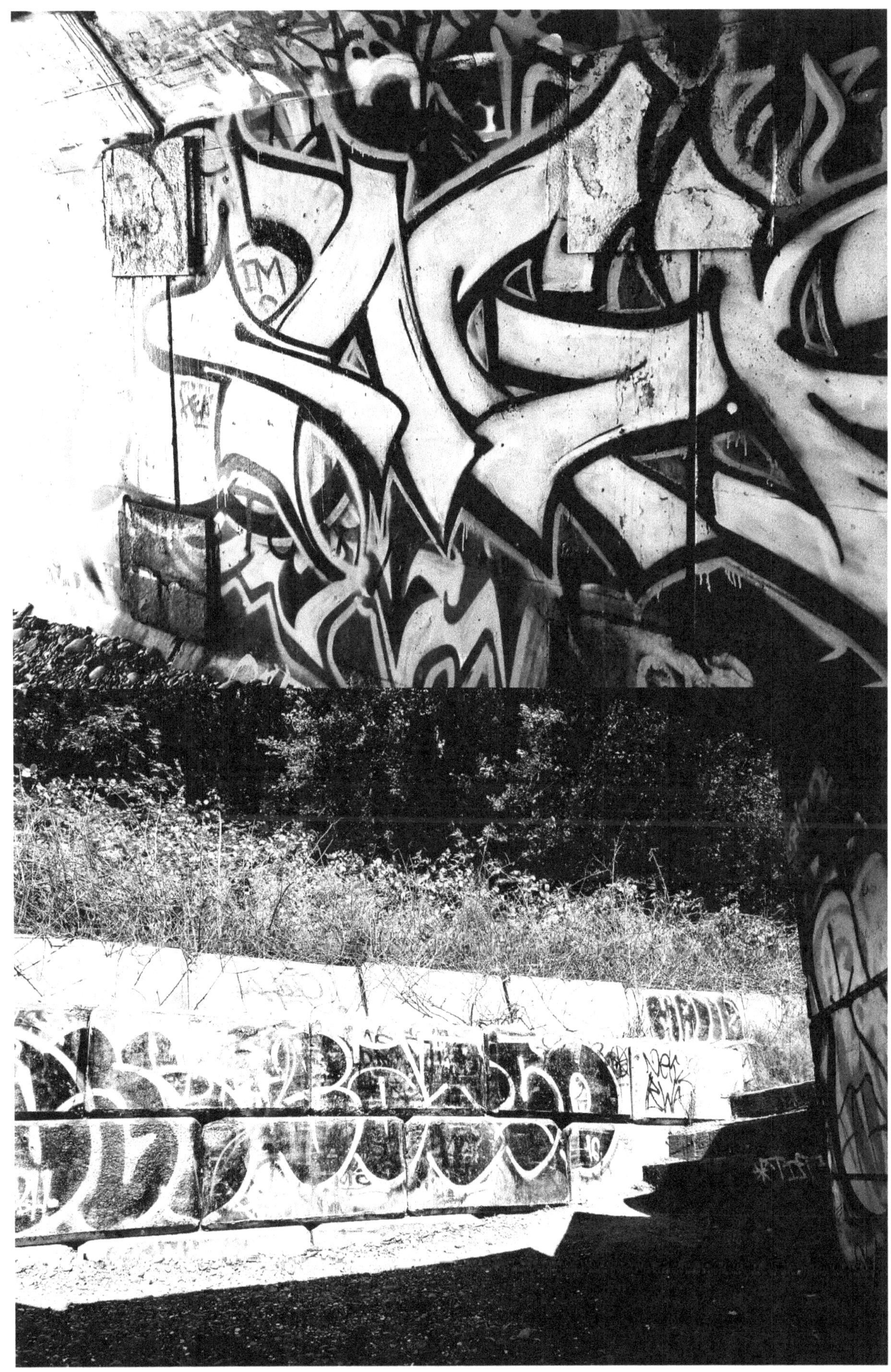

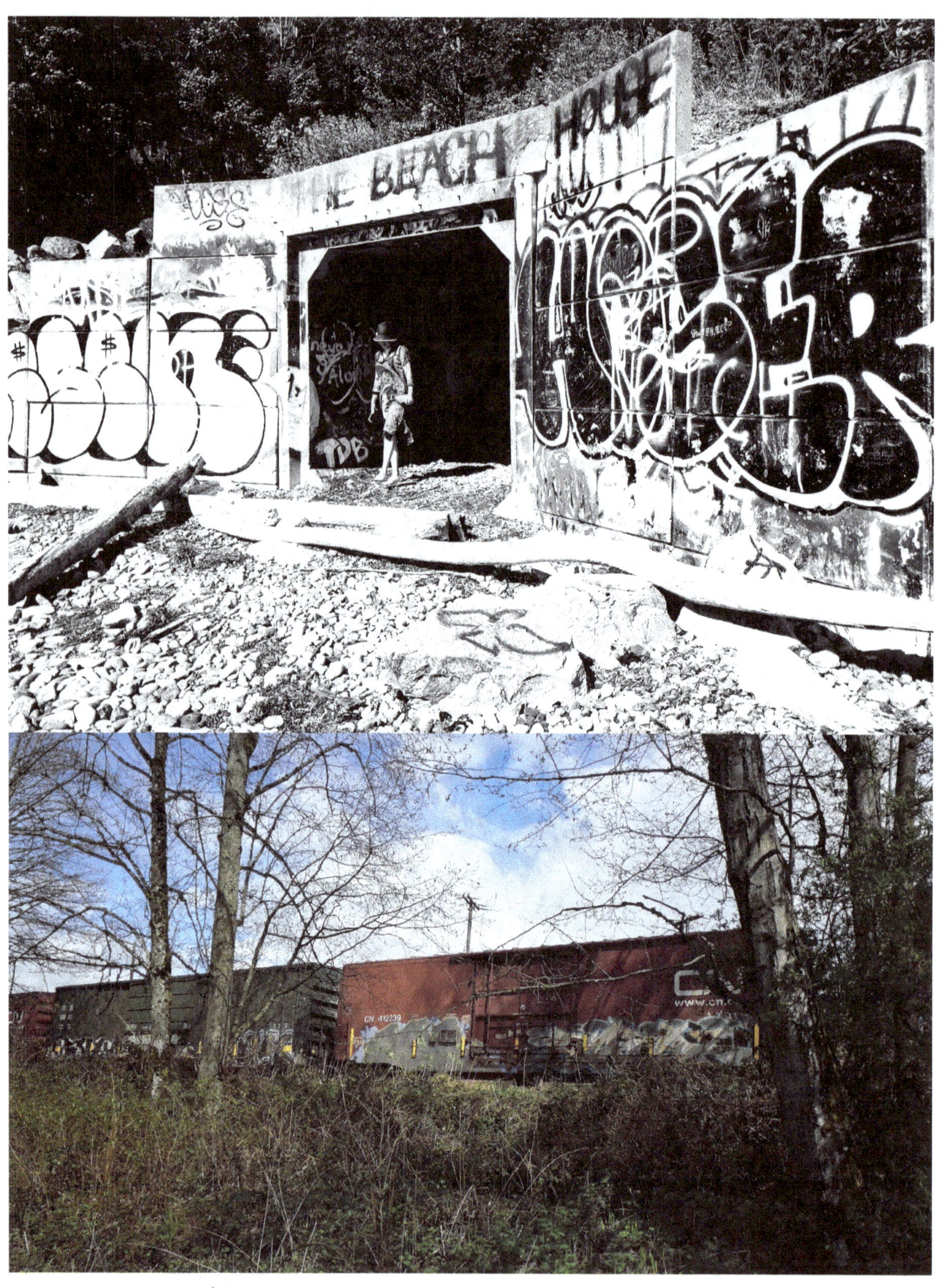

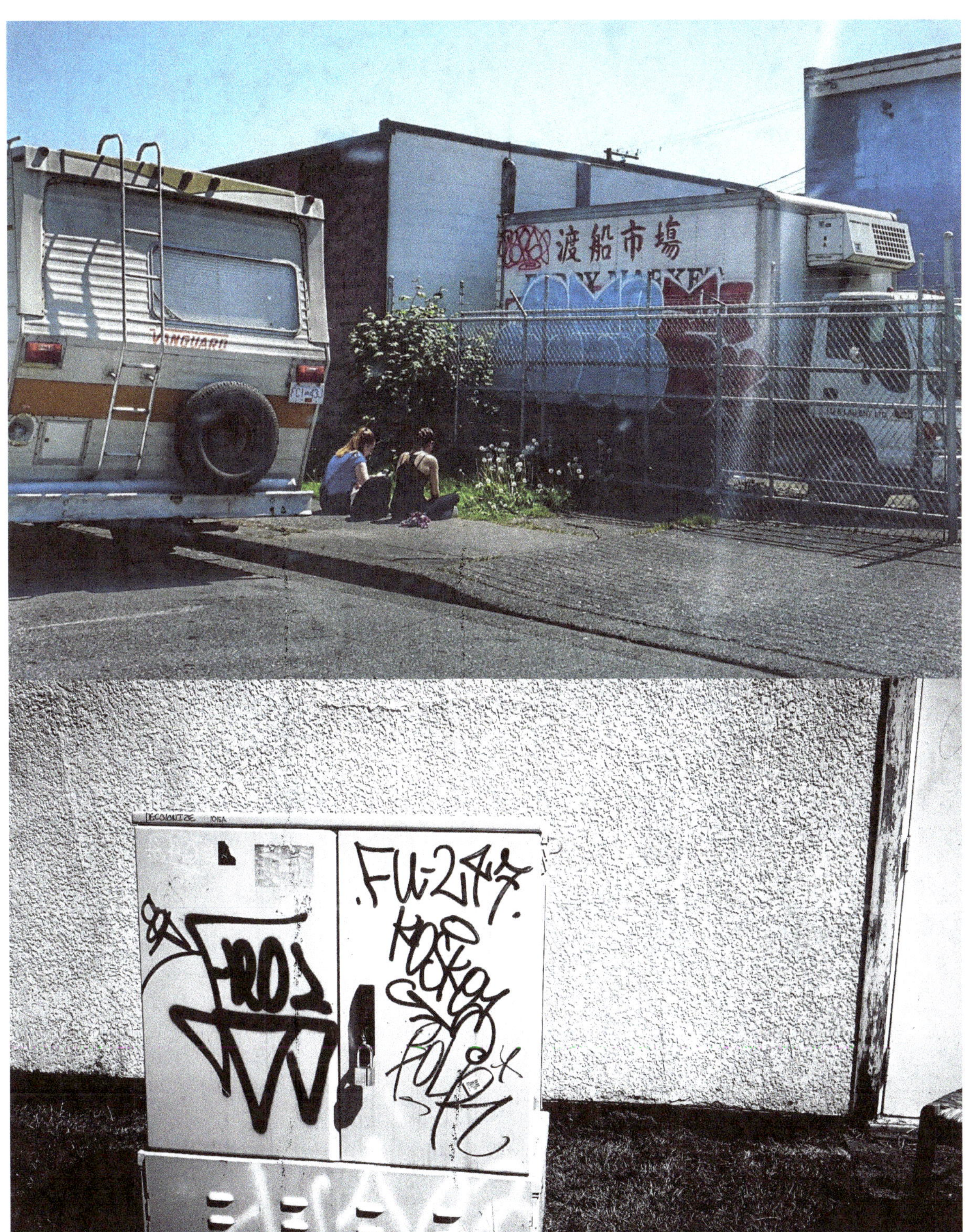

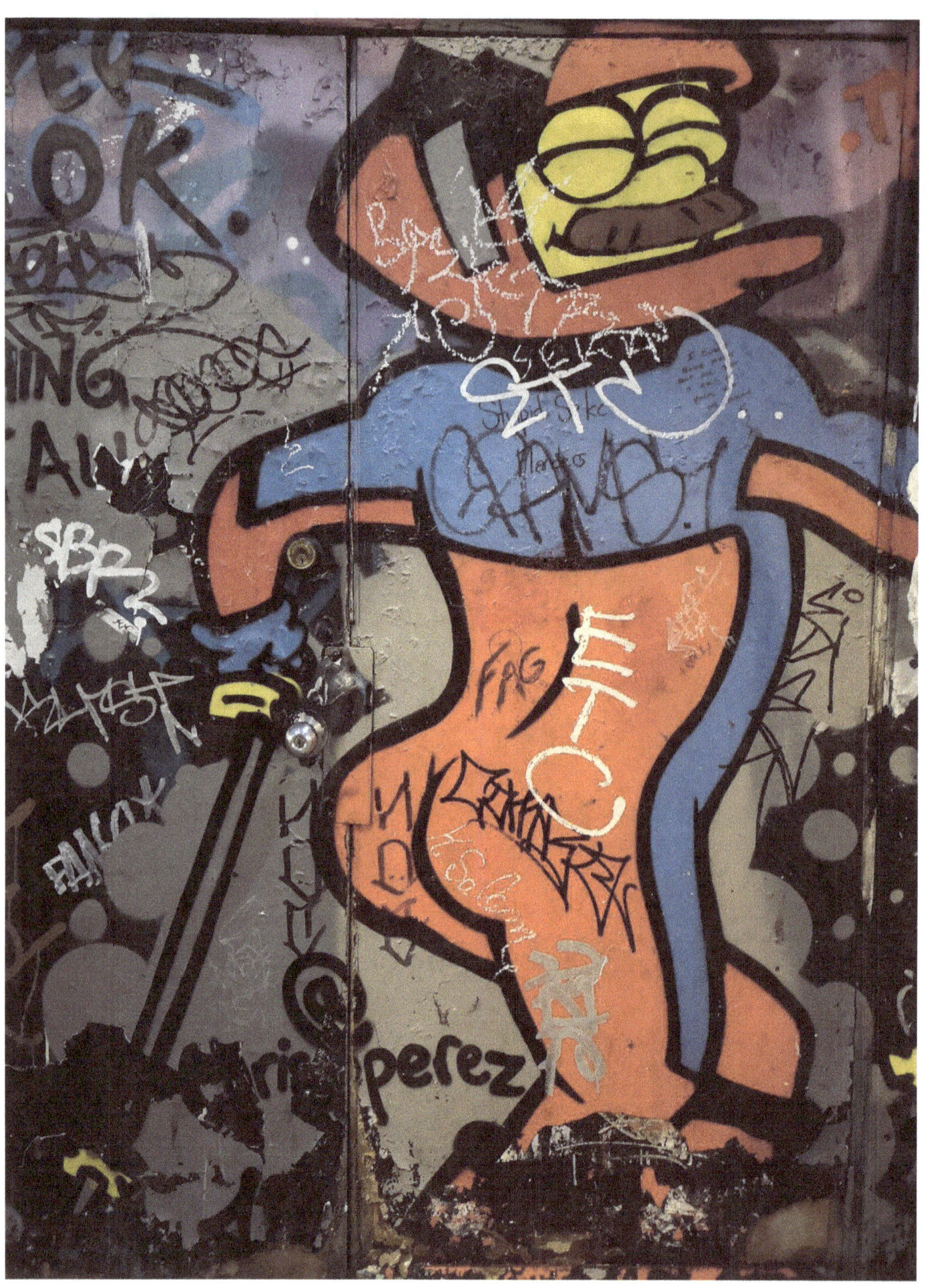

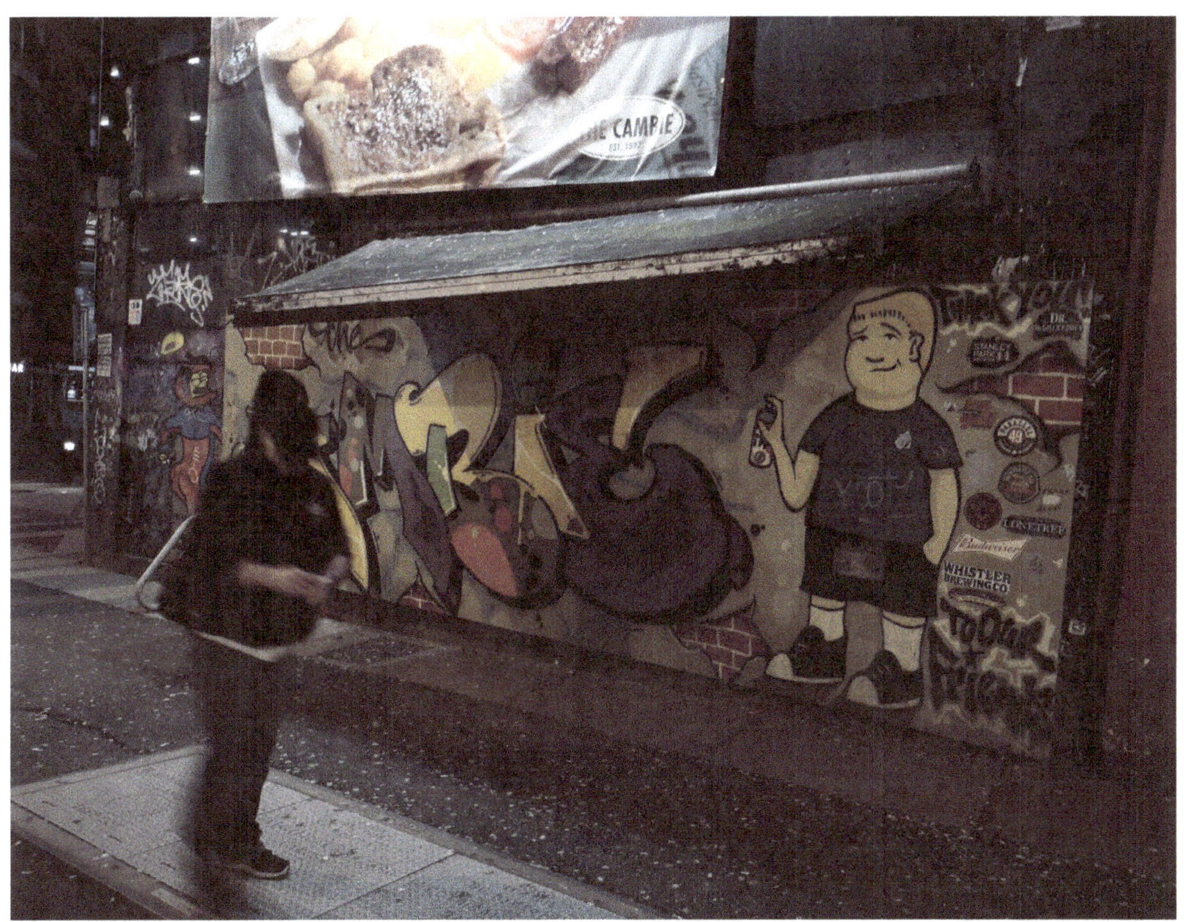

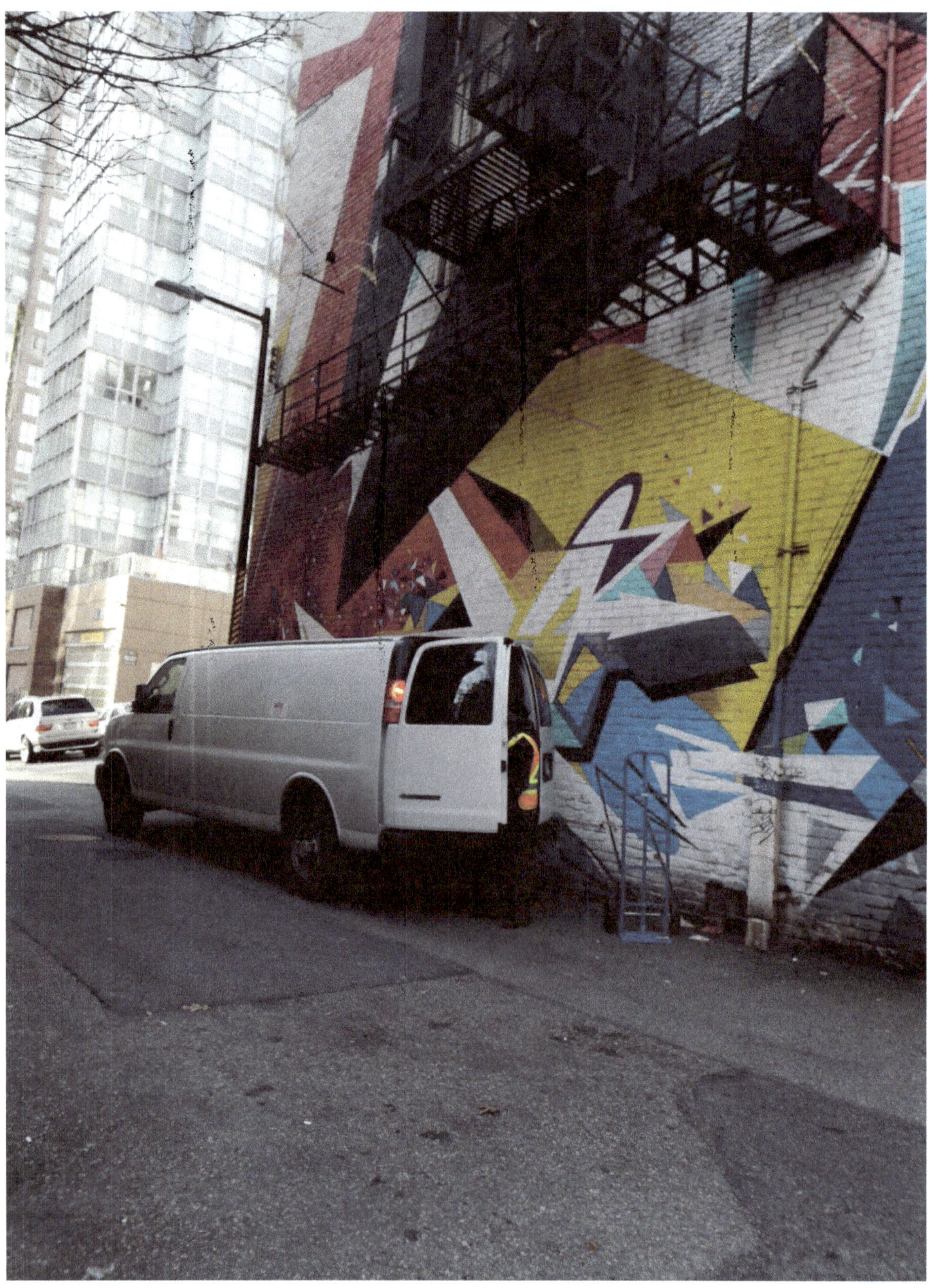

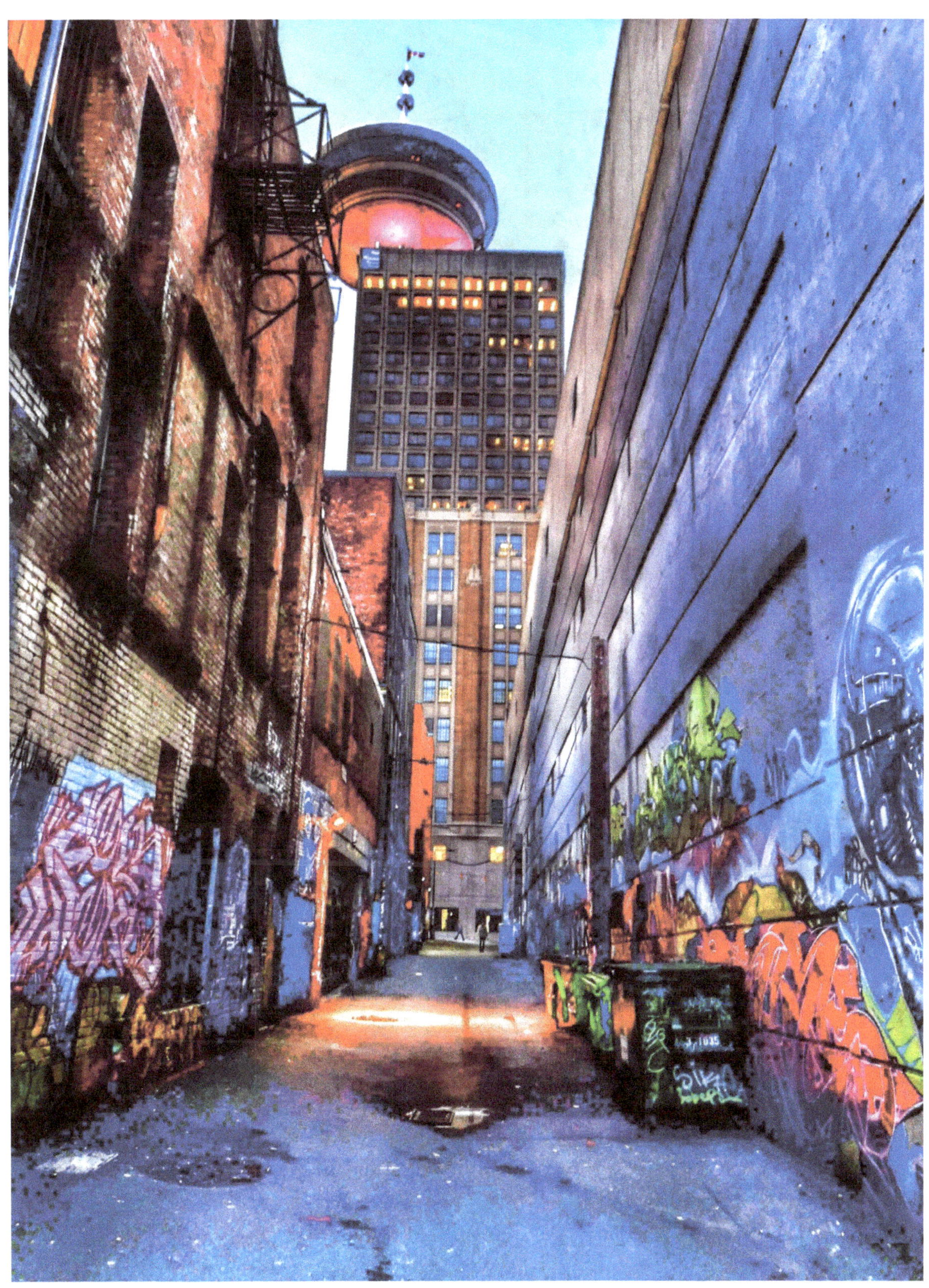

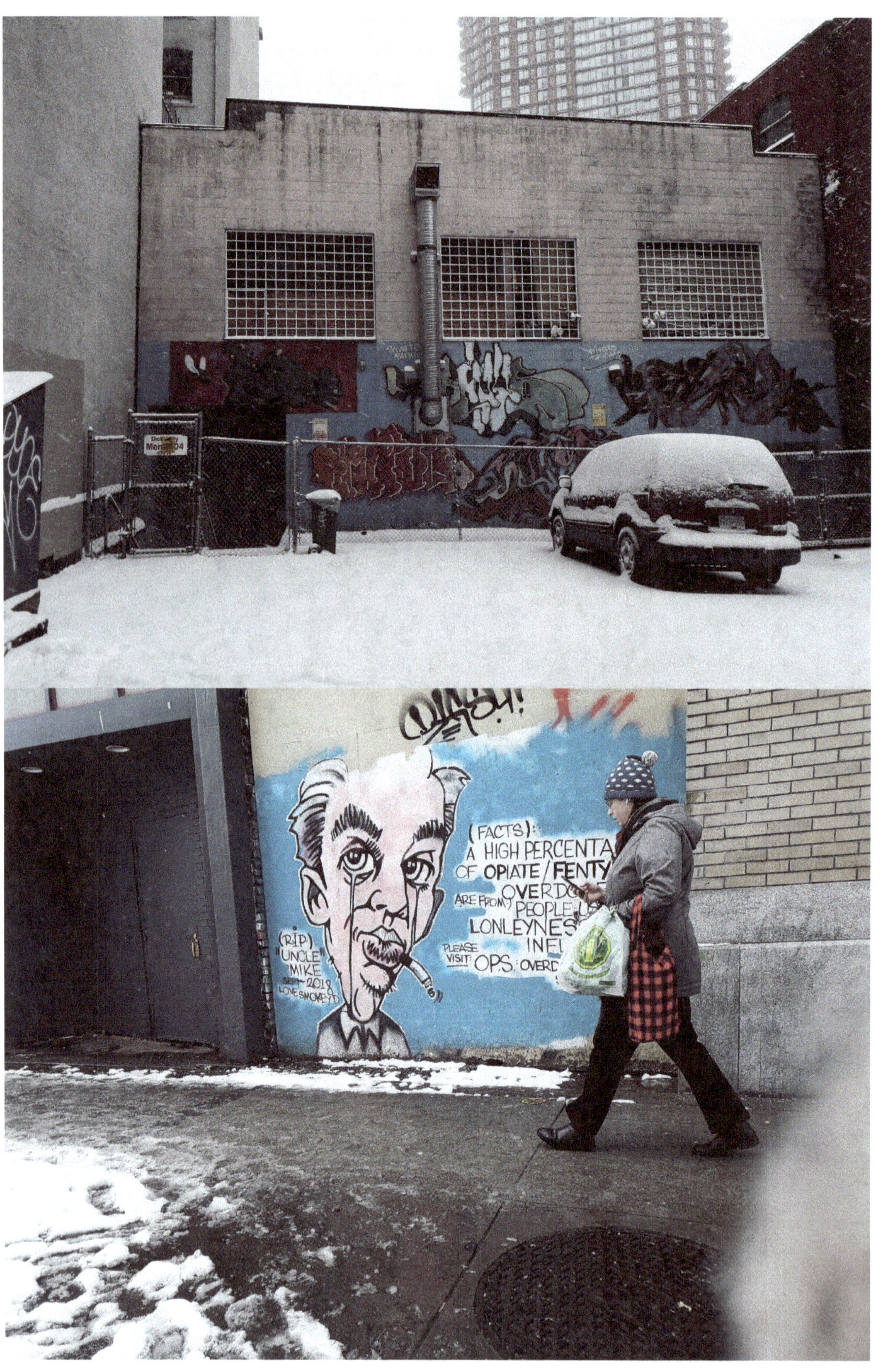
(FACTS):
A HIGH PERCENTA
OF OPIATE / FENTY
ARE FROM) OVERD
PEOPLE
LONLEYNES
IN F!
PLEASE
VISIT: O.P.S. OVERD
(R.I.P.)
"UNCLE"
MIKE
SEPT 2018
LOVE SMOKEY D

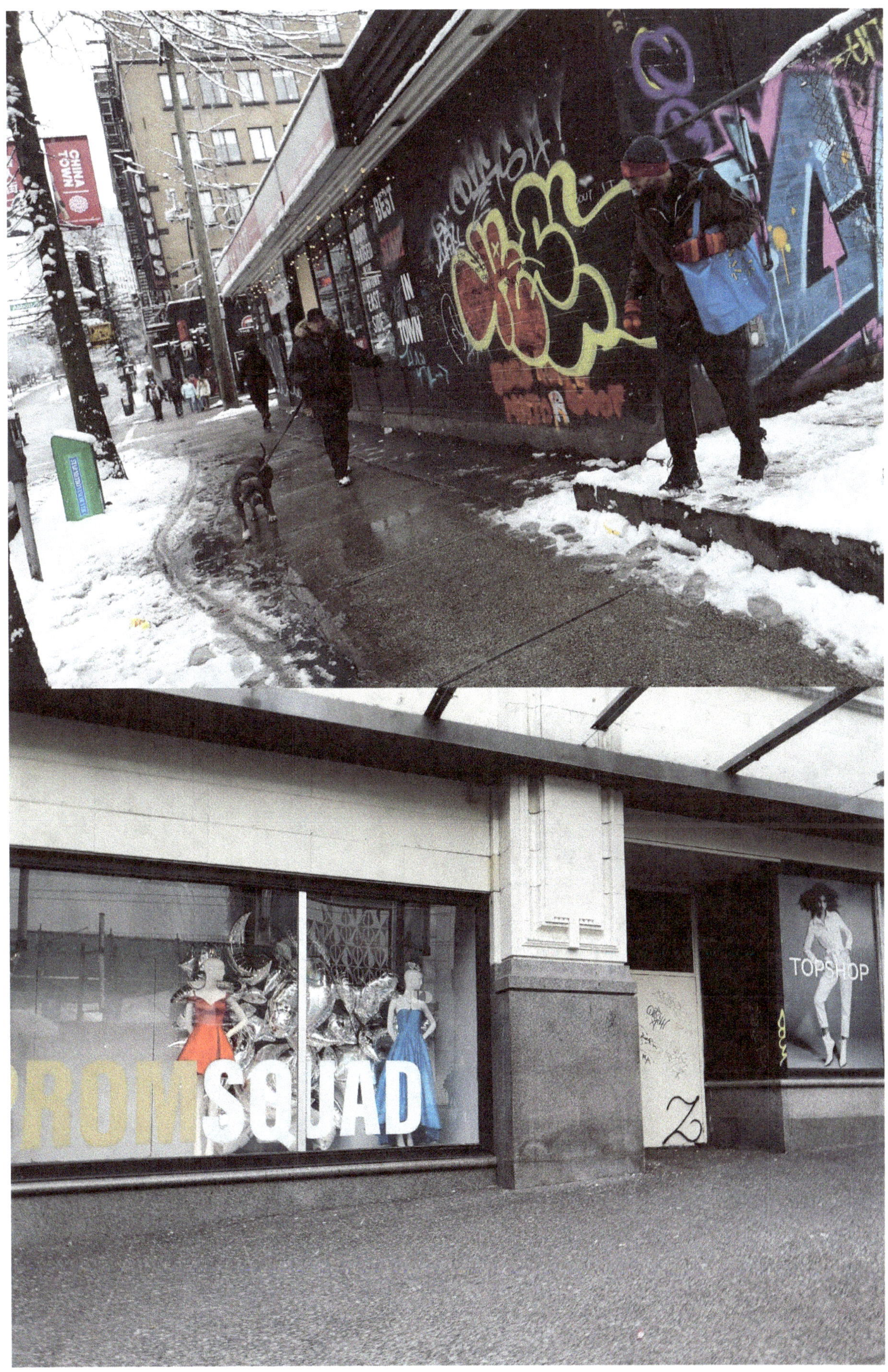
CHINA TOWN
BEST
IN TOWN
PROMSQUAD
TOPSHOP

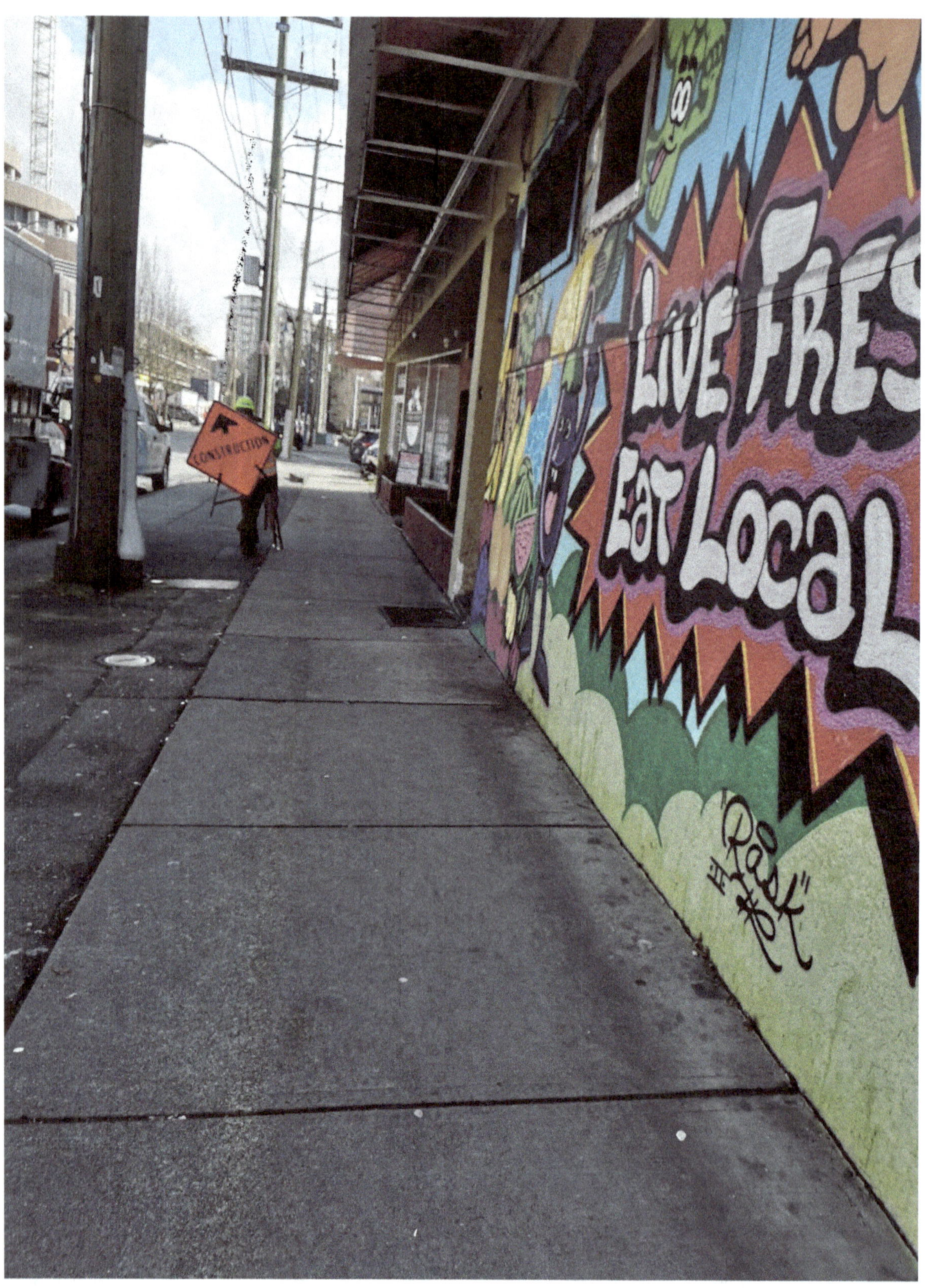

CONSTRUCCION
LIVE FRES
Eat Local

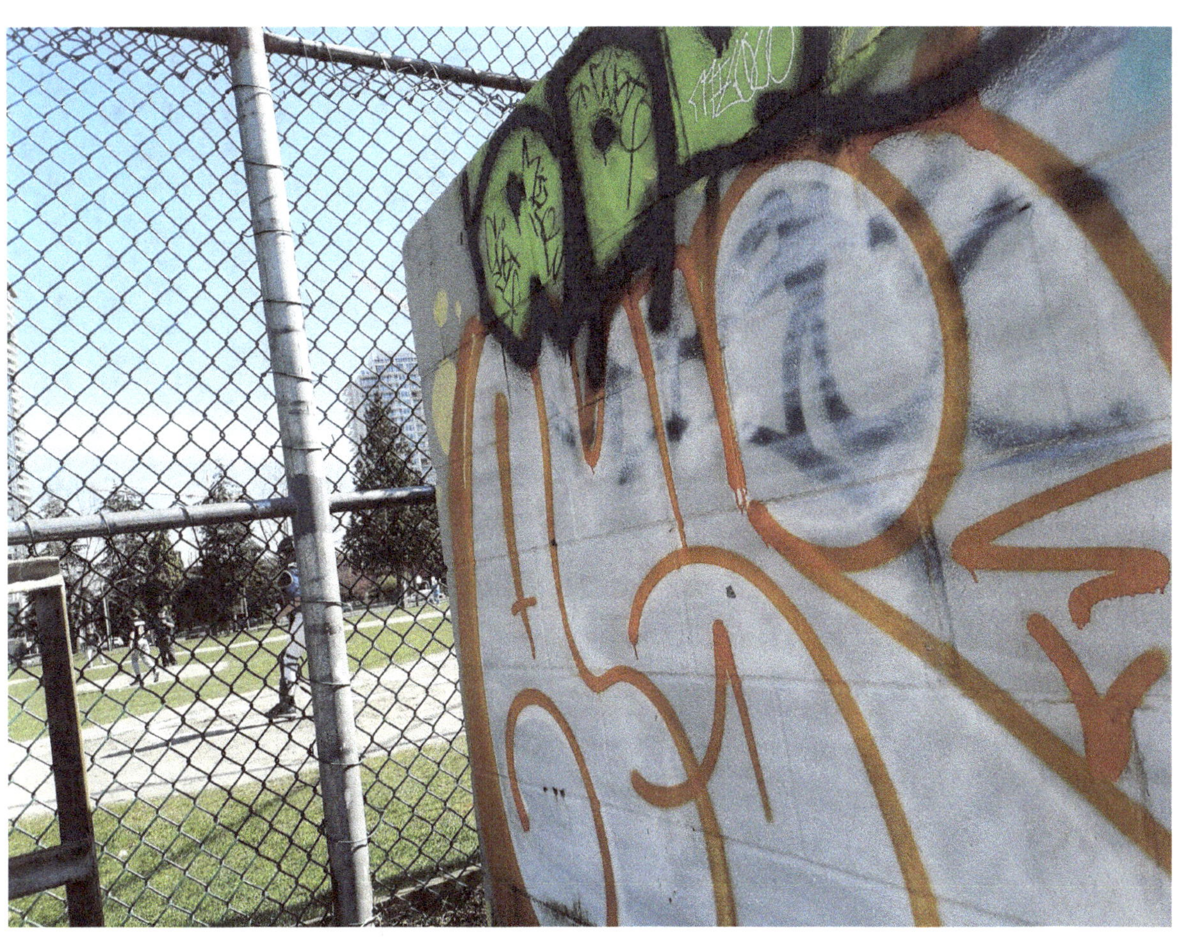

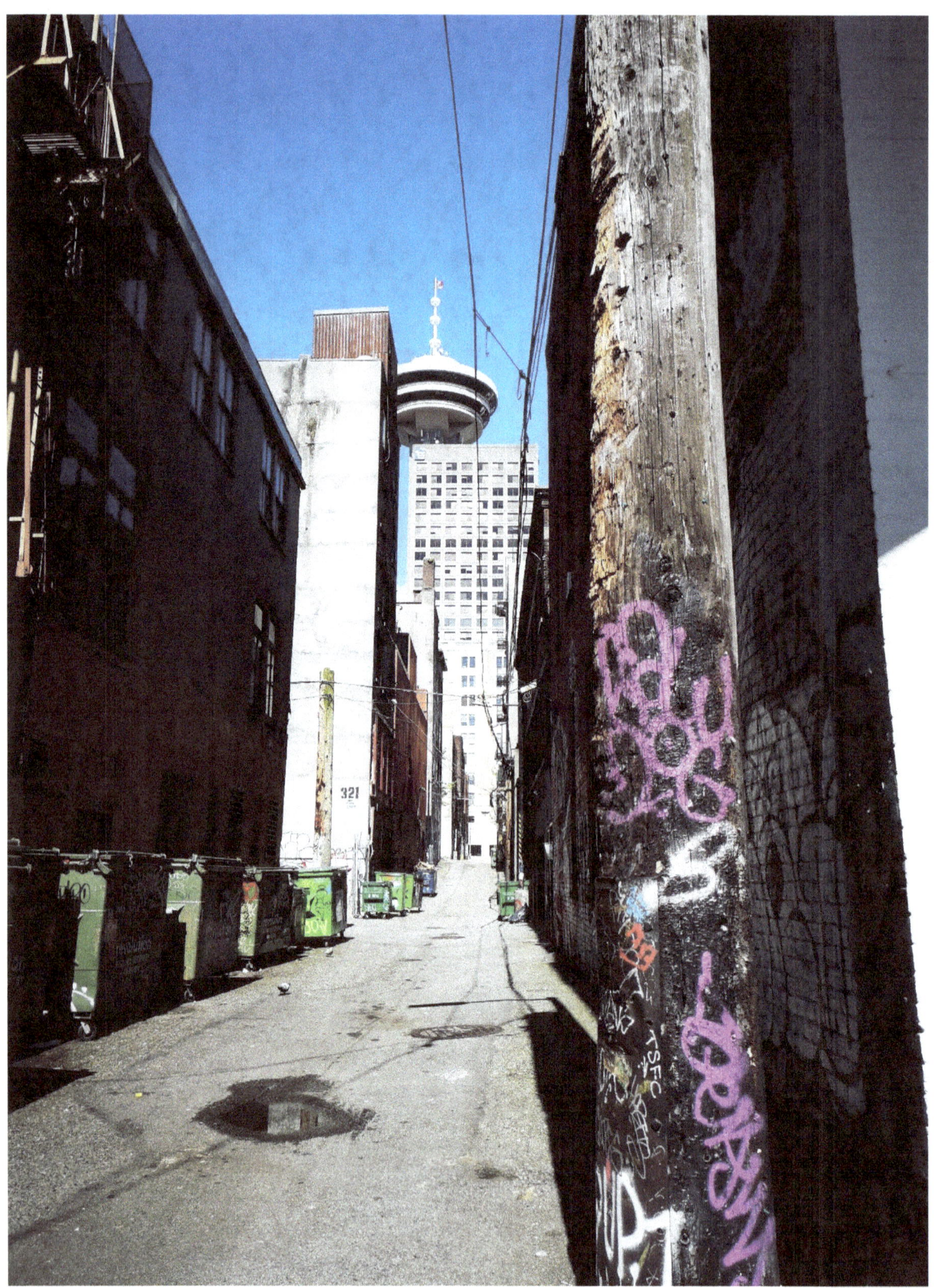
321
TSFC

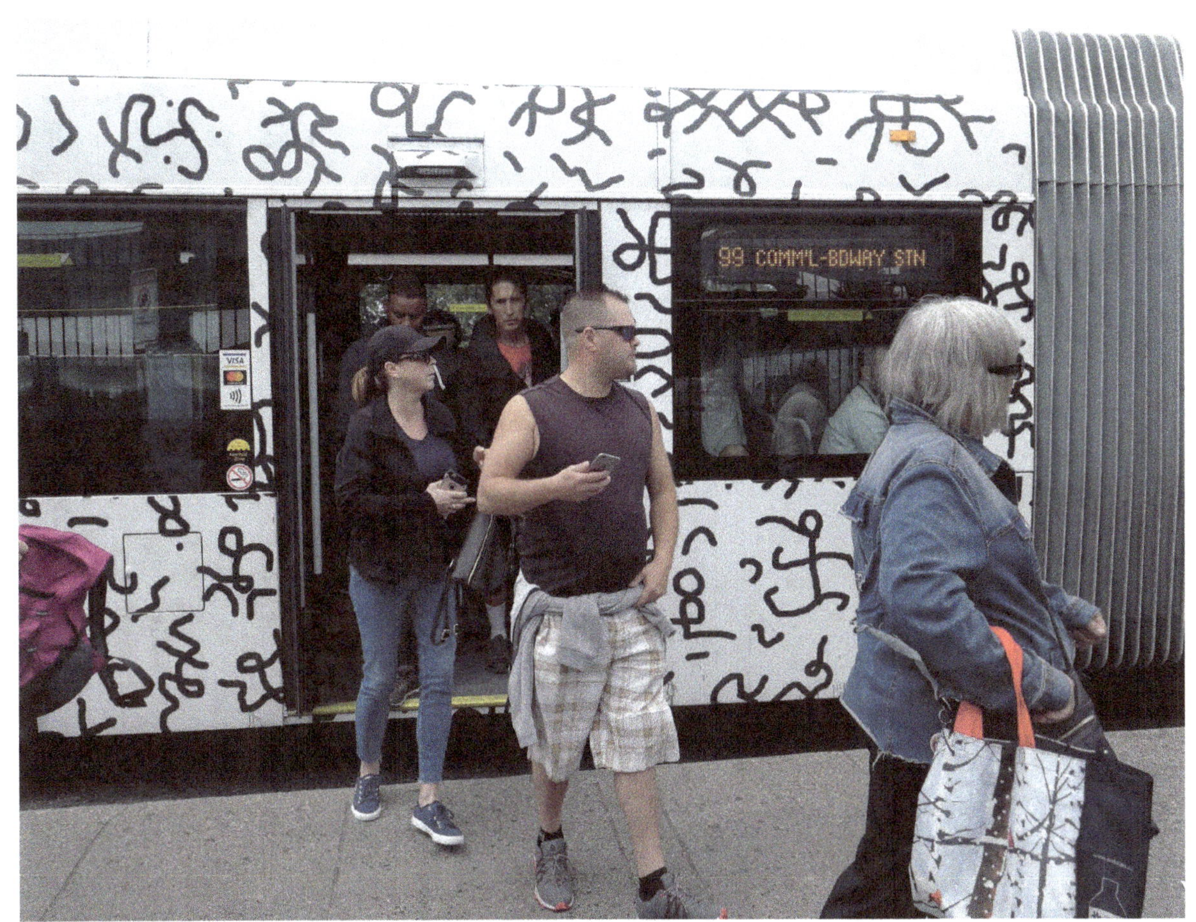

99 COMM'L-BDWAY STN

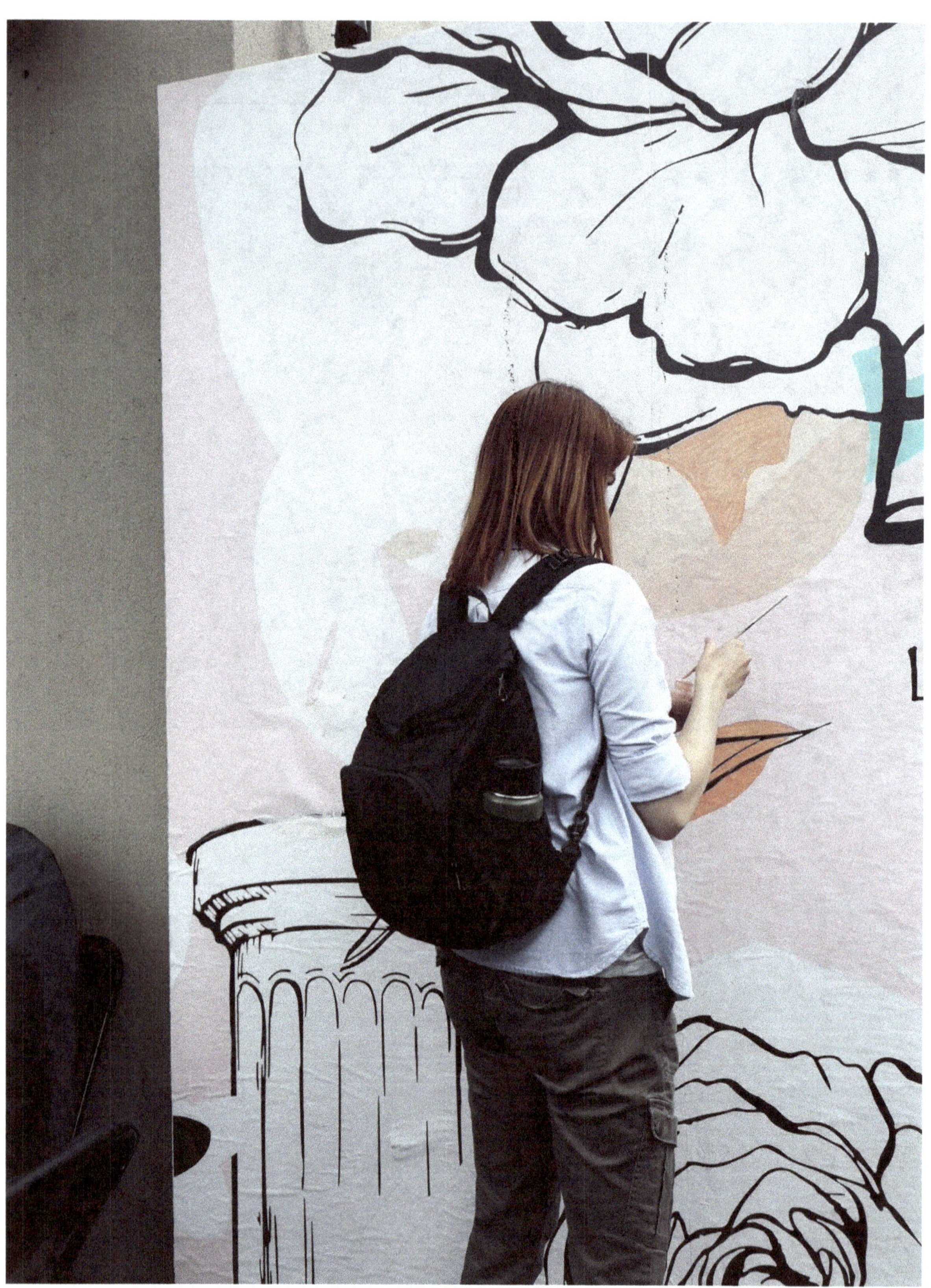

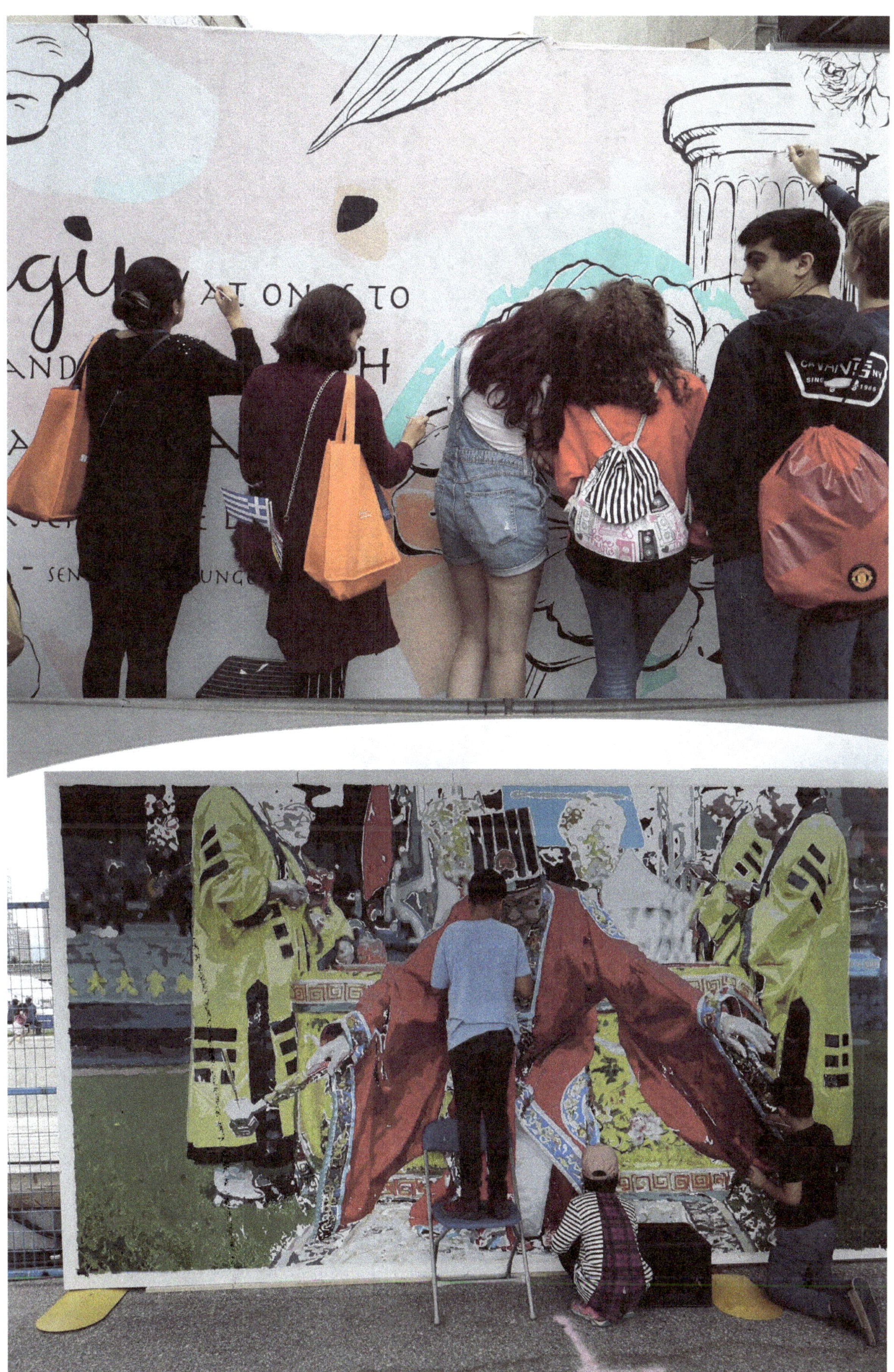

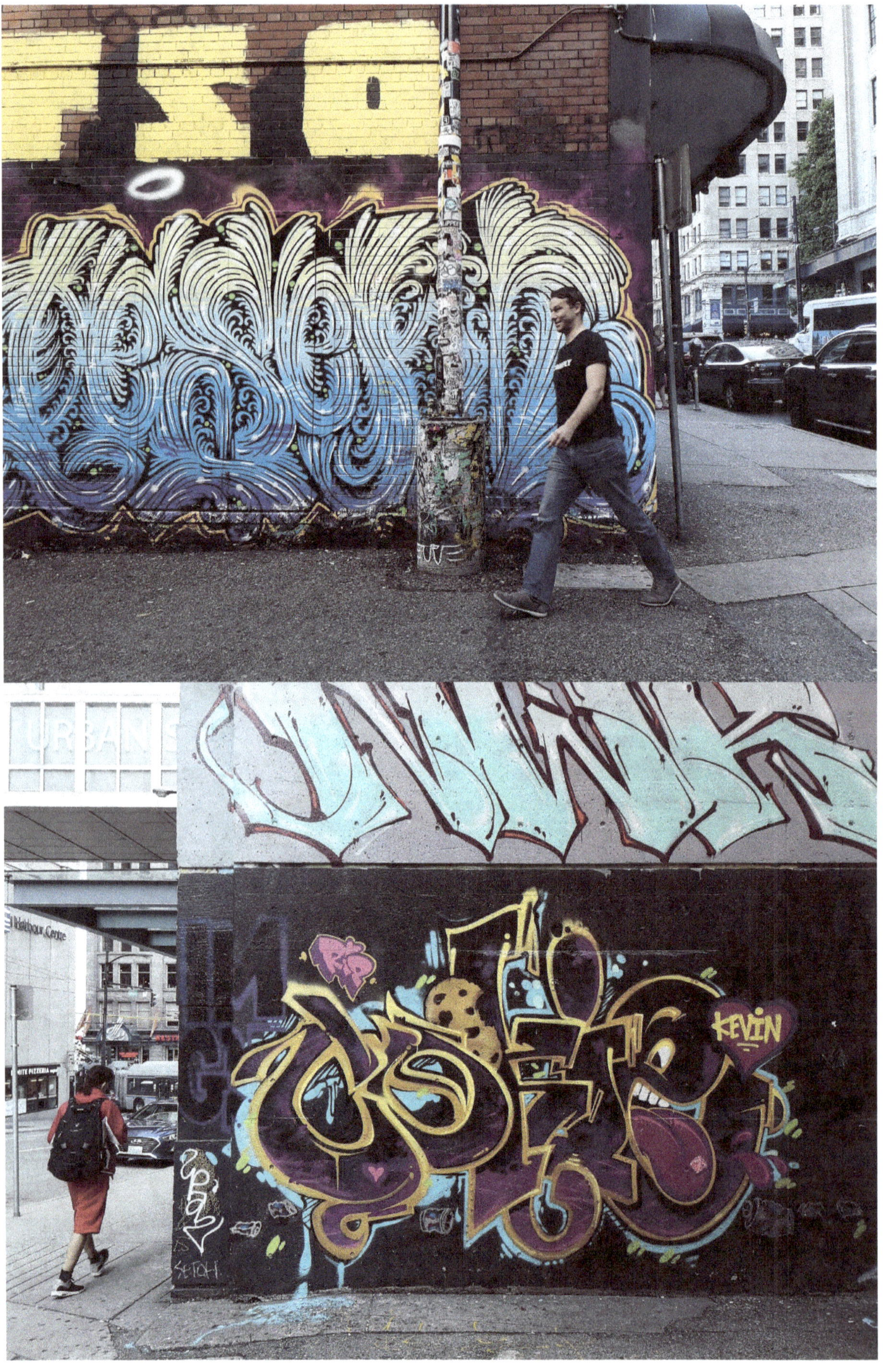

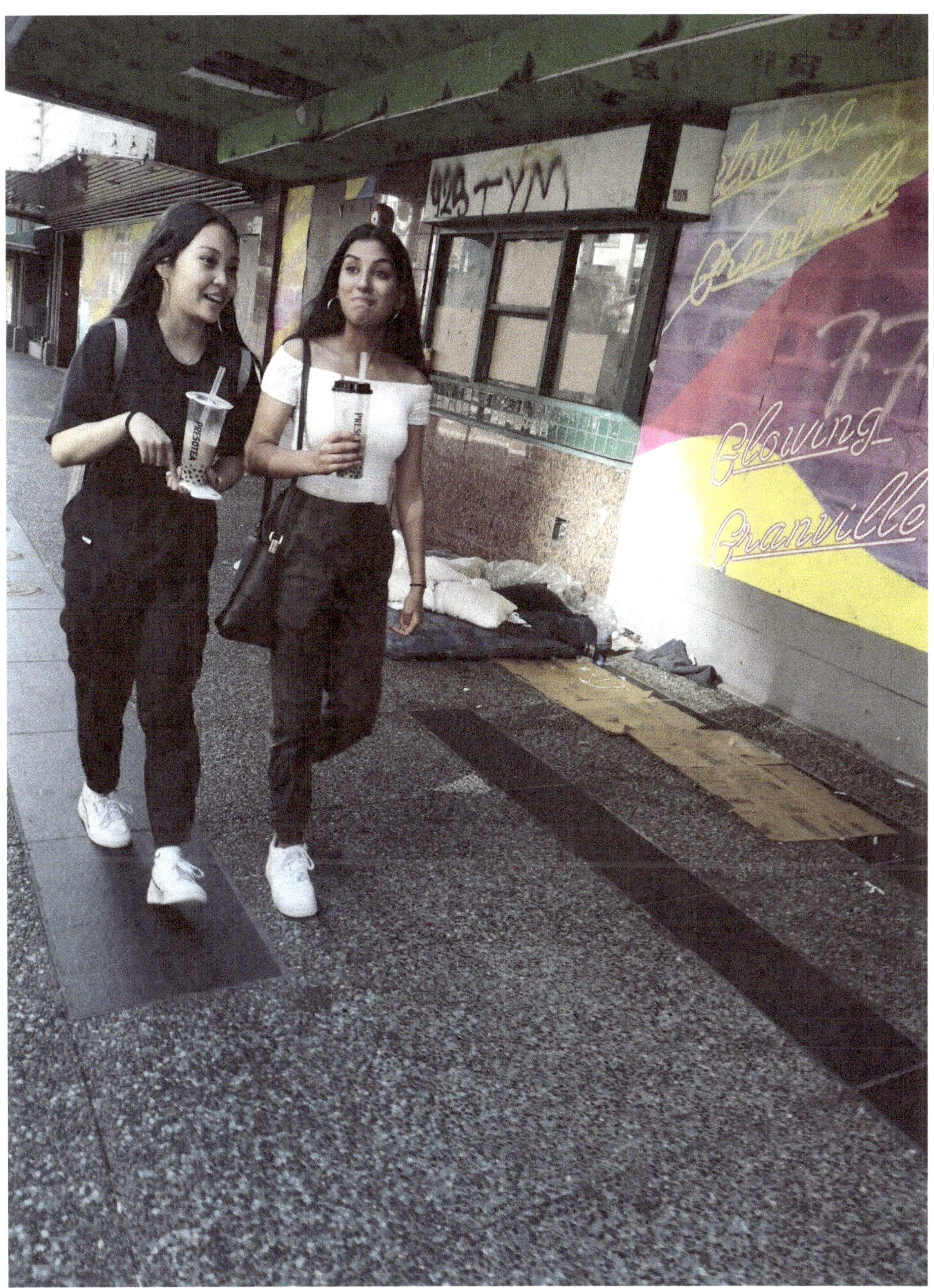
Glowing
Granville
Glowing
Granville
PRESOTEA
PRESOTEA

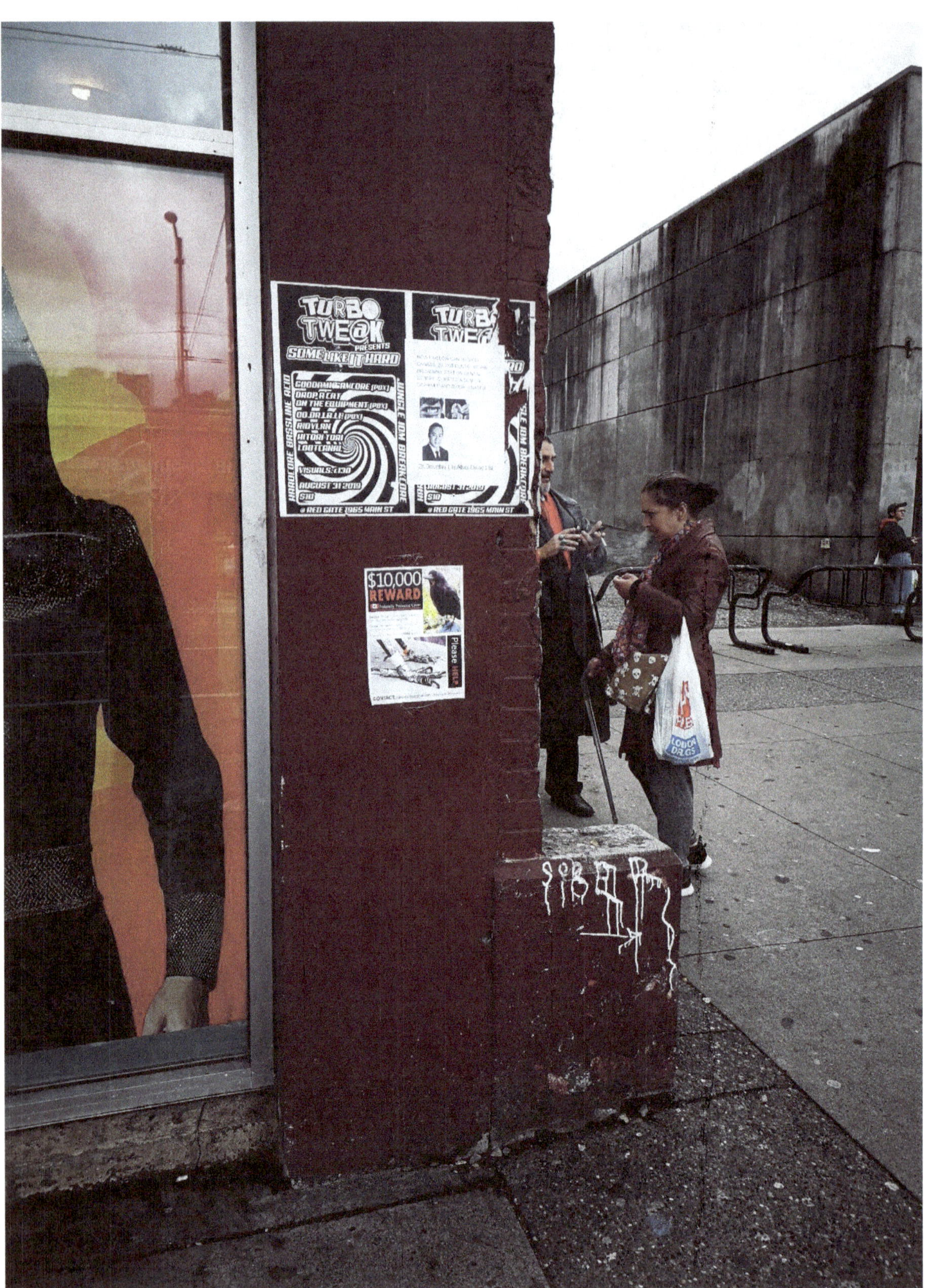

TURBO TWE@K
PRESENTS
SOME LIKE IT HARD
HARDCORE BASSLINE ACID
GOODNAMEGAMCORE (PDX)
DROP A CAT
ON THE EQUIPMENT (PDX)
DO.DA.LA.LH (PDX)
RIDYLAN
HITORI TORI
LOOTCANAL
JUNGLE IDM BREAKCORE
VISUALS: ZILD
AUGUST 31 2019
$10
@ RED GATE 1965 MAIN ST
TURBO TWE@K
AUGUST 31 2019
$10
@ RED GATE 1965 MAIN ST
$10,000
REWARD
Please HELP

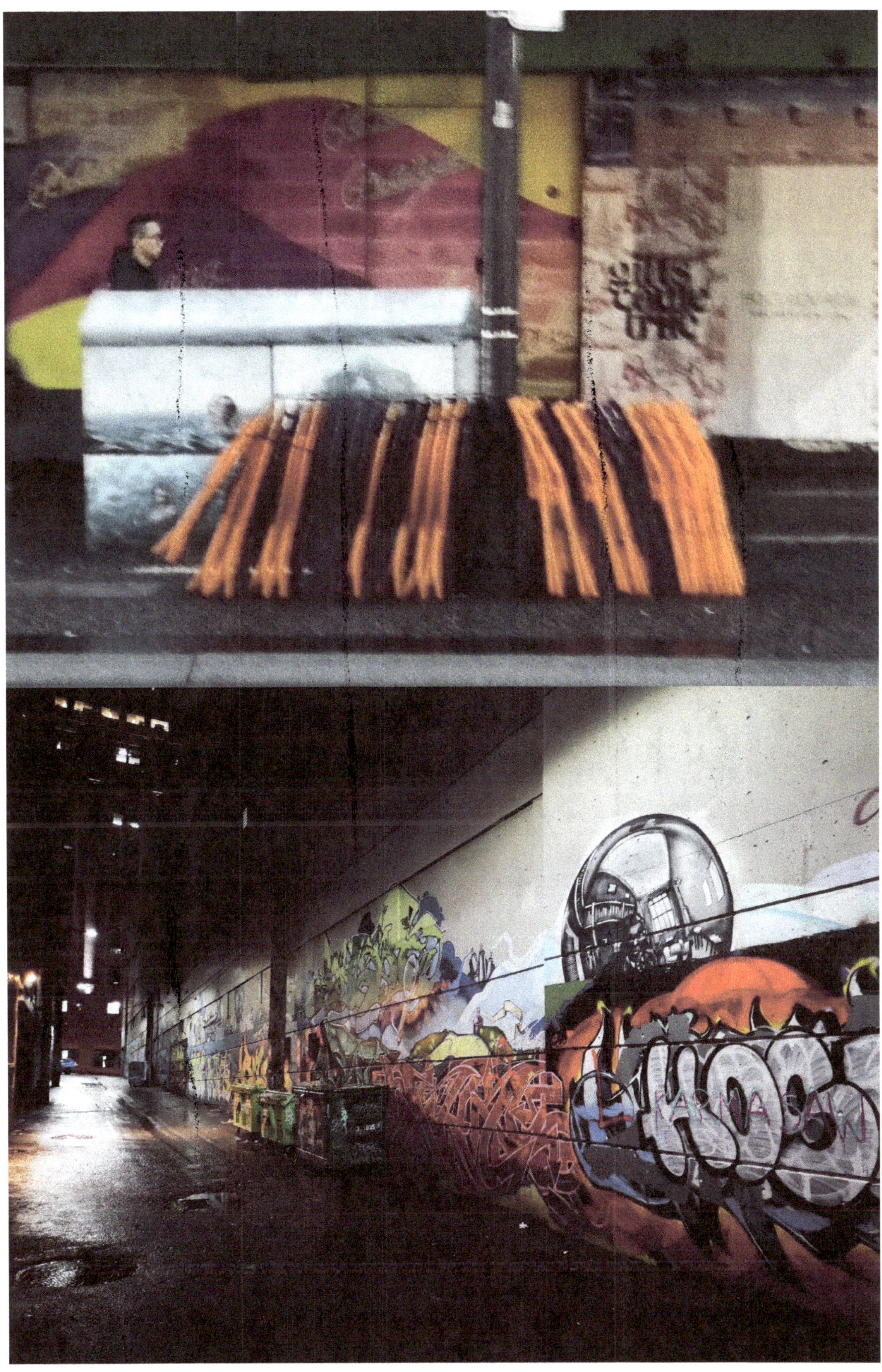

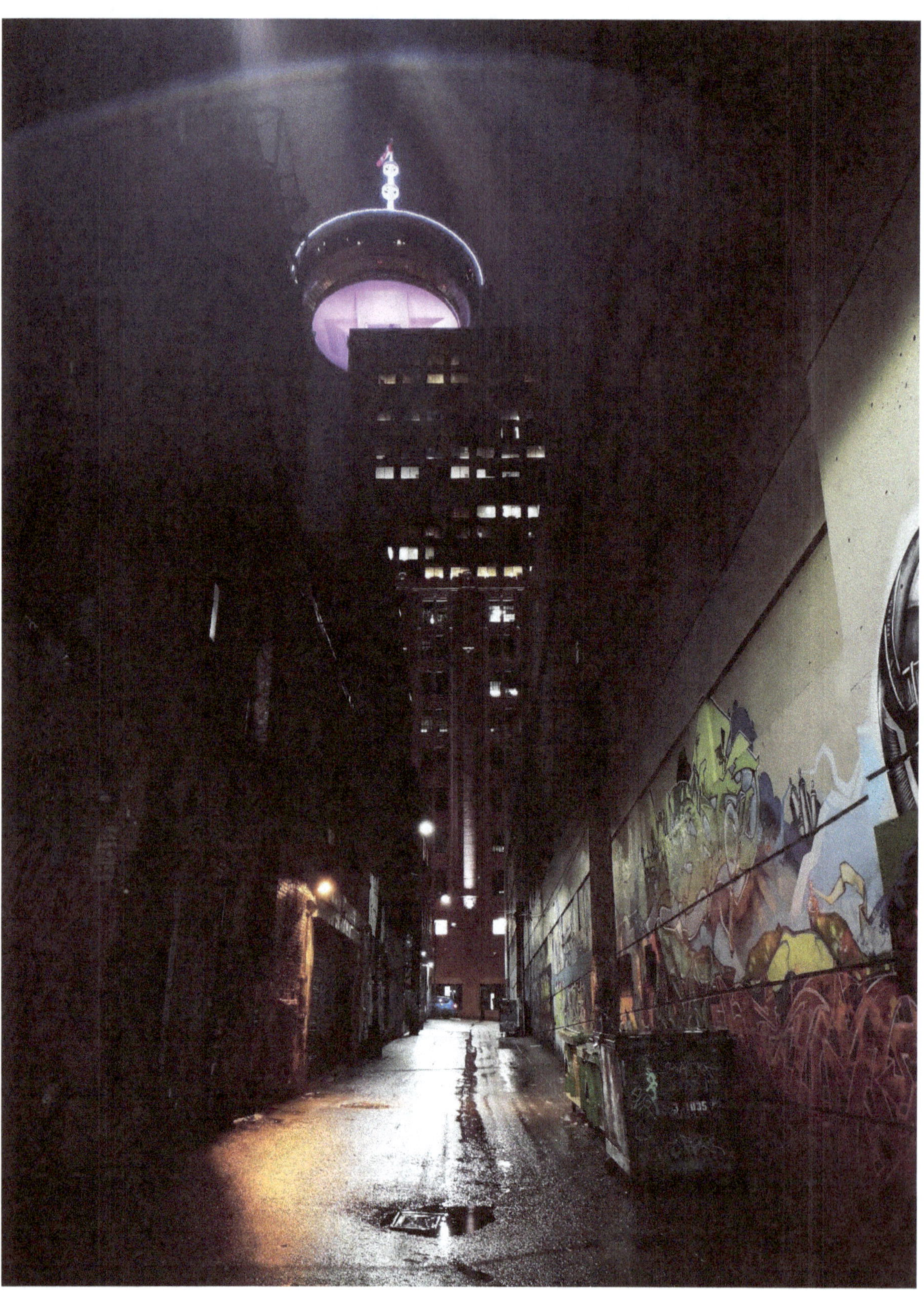

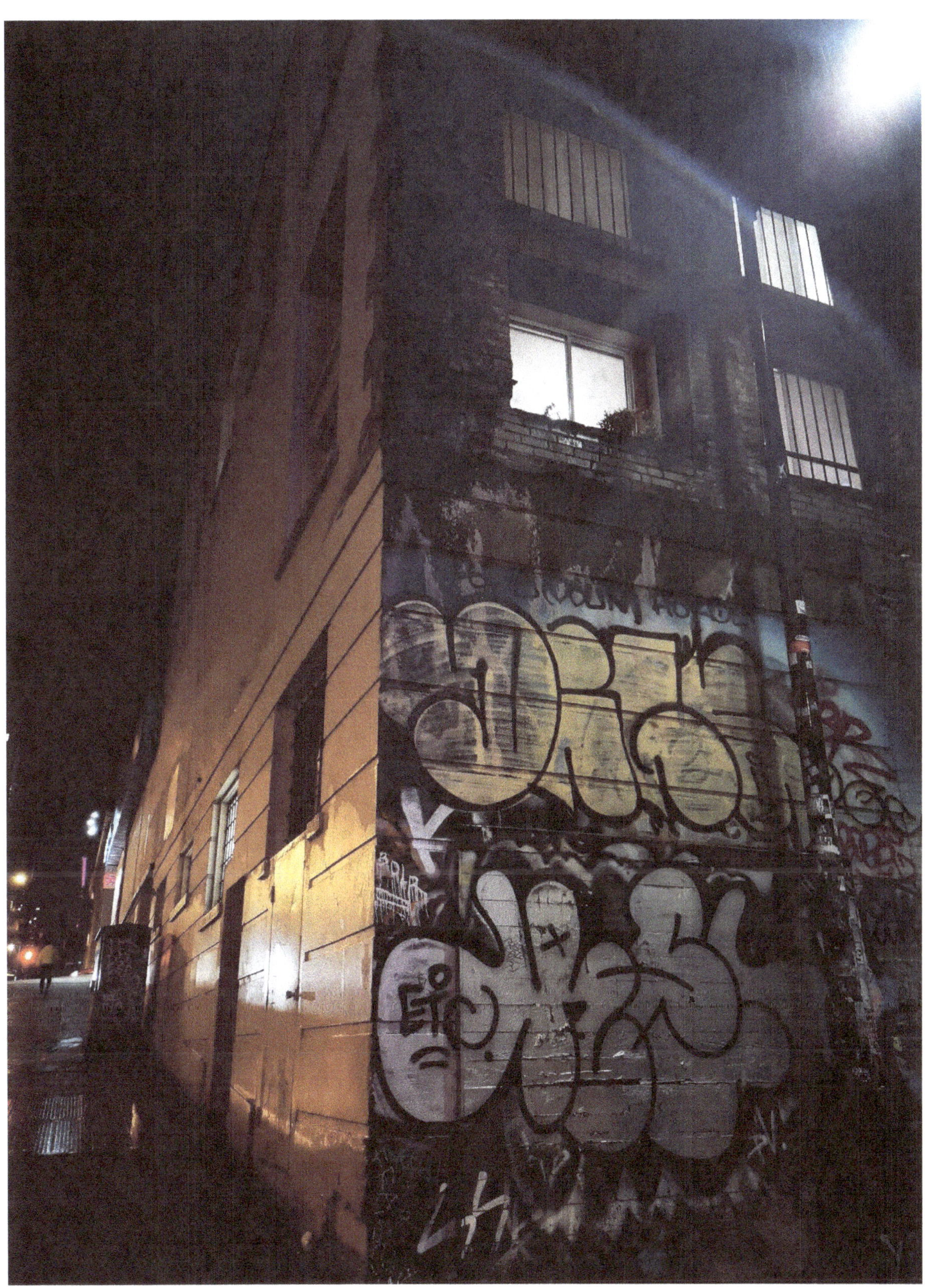

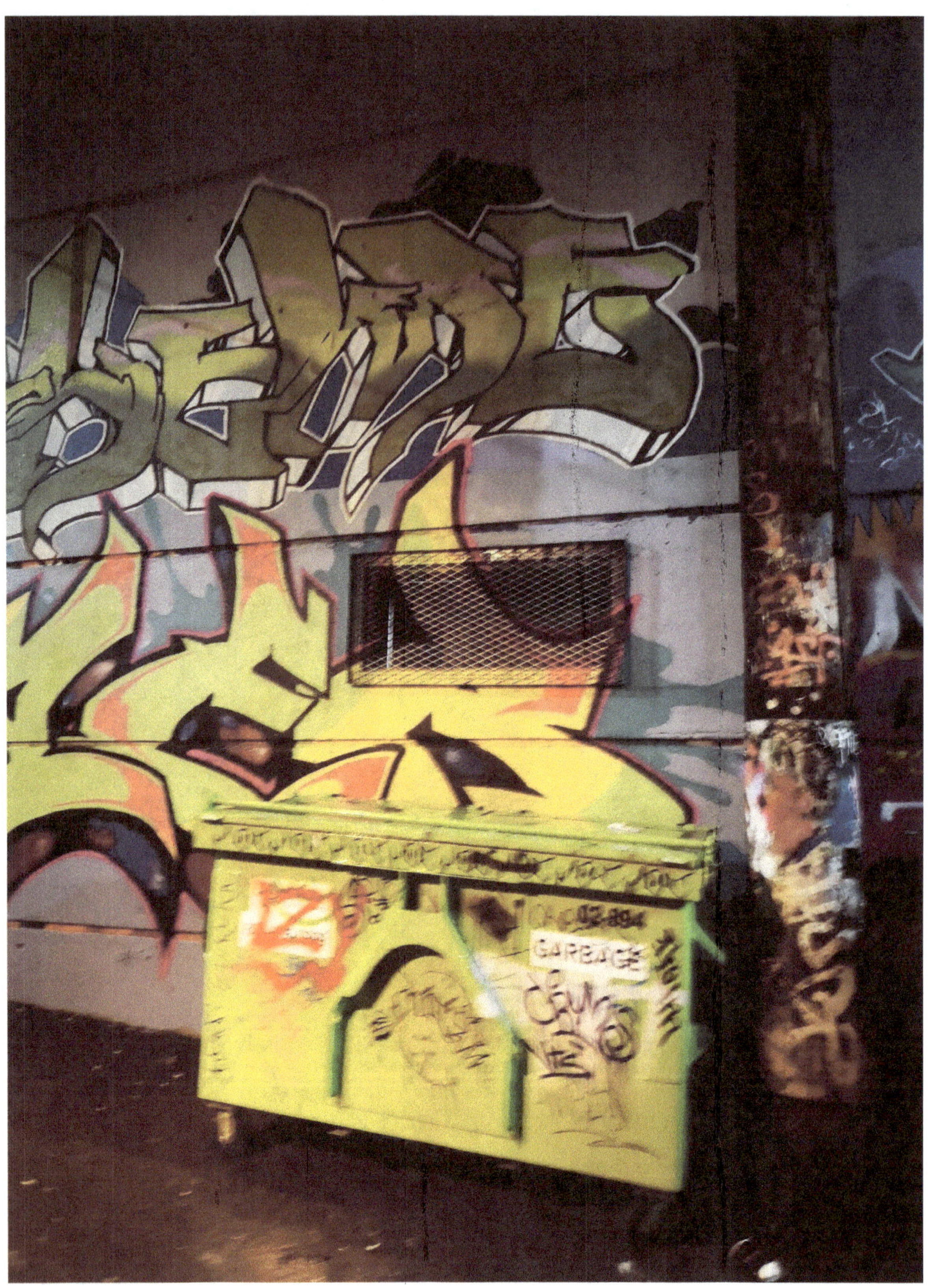

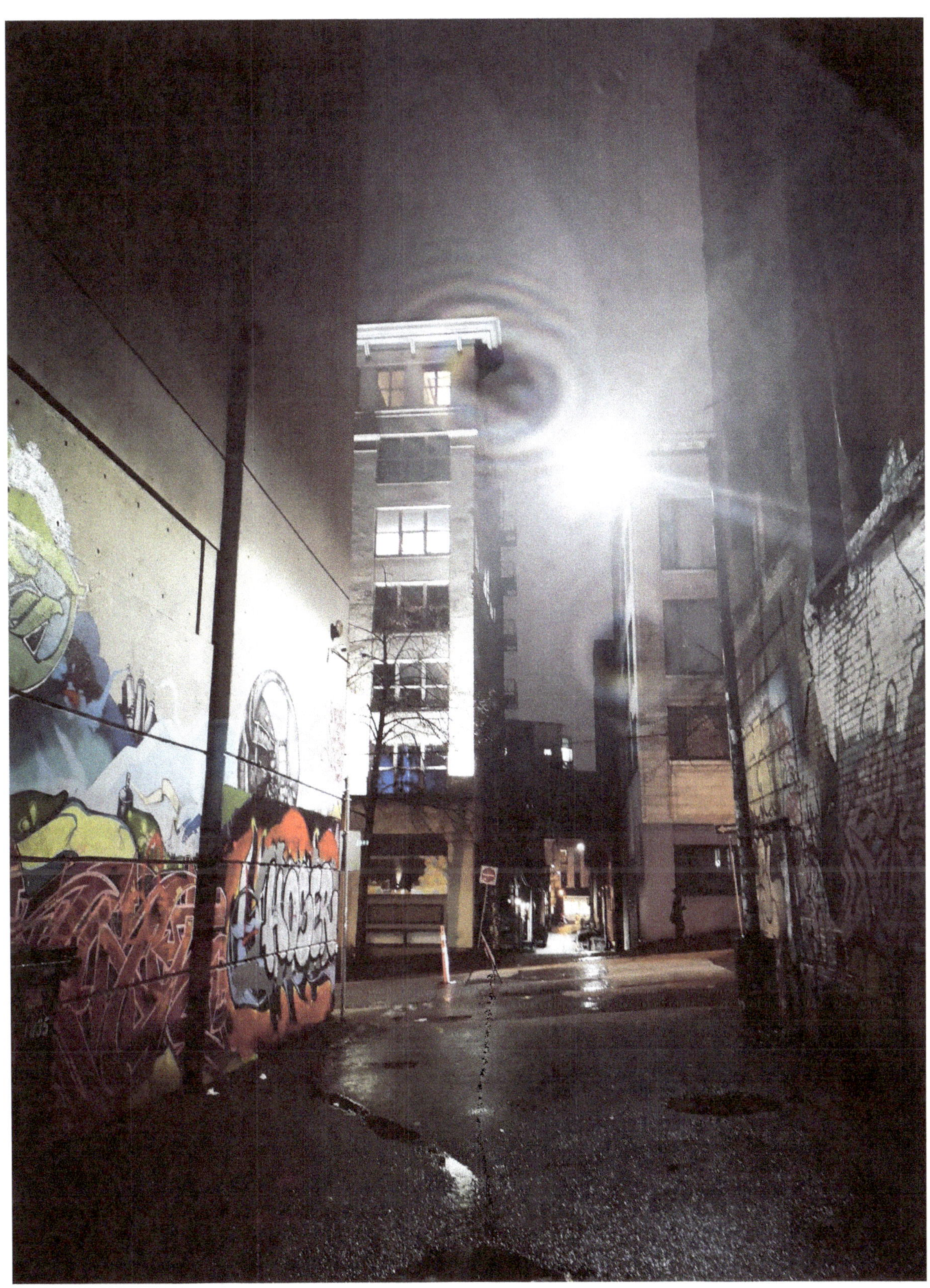

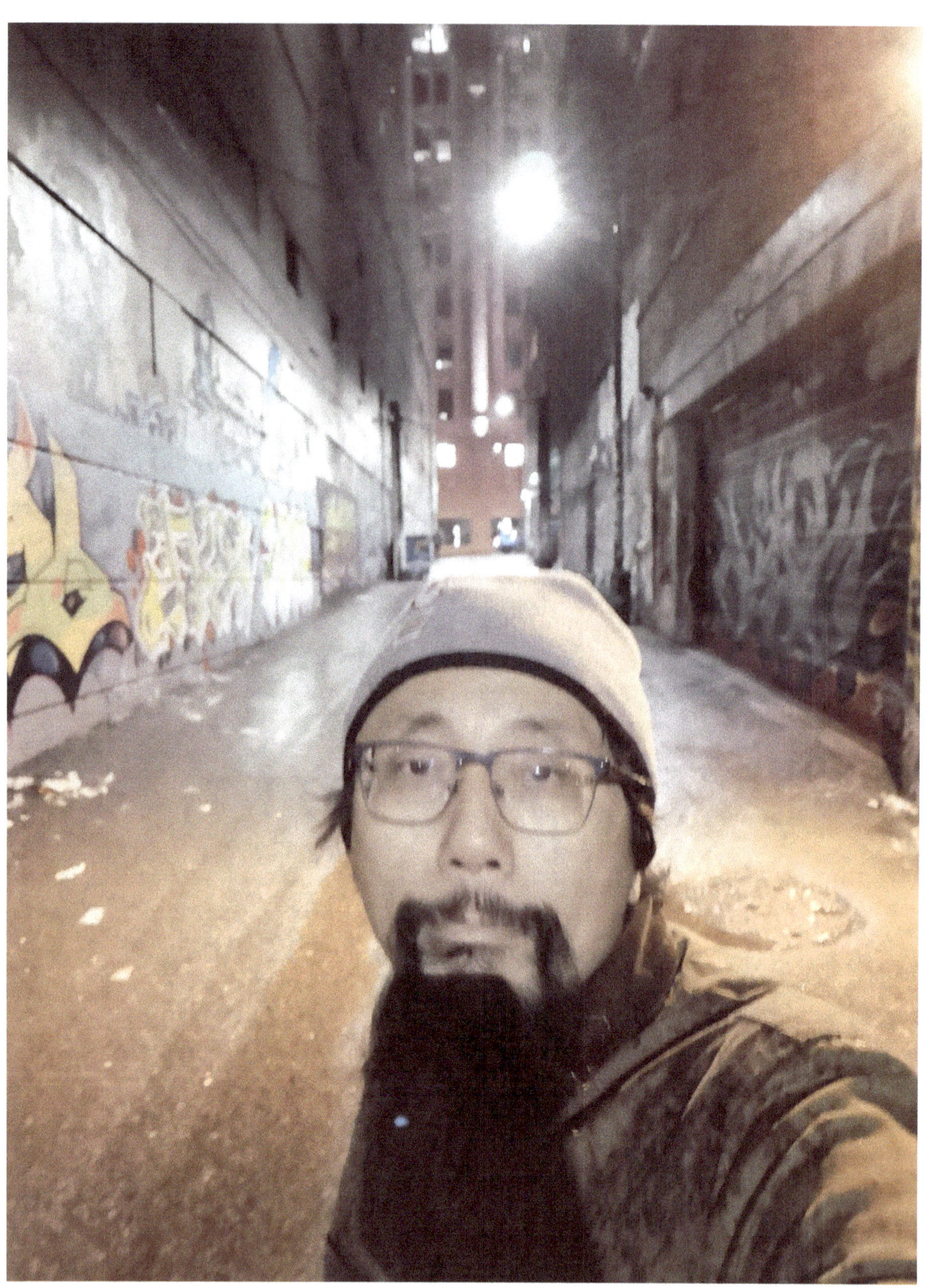

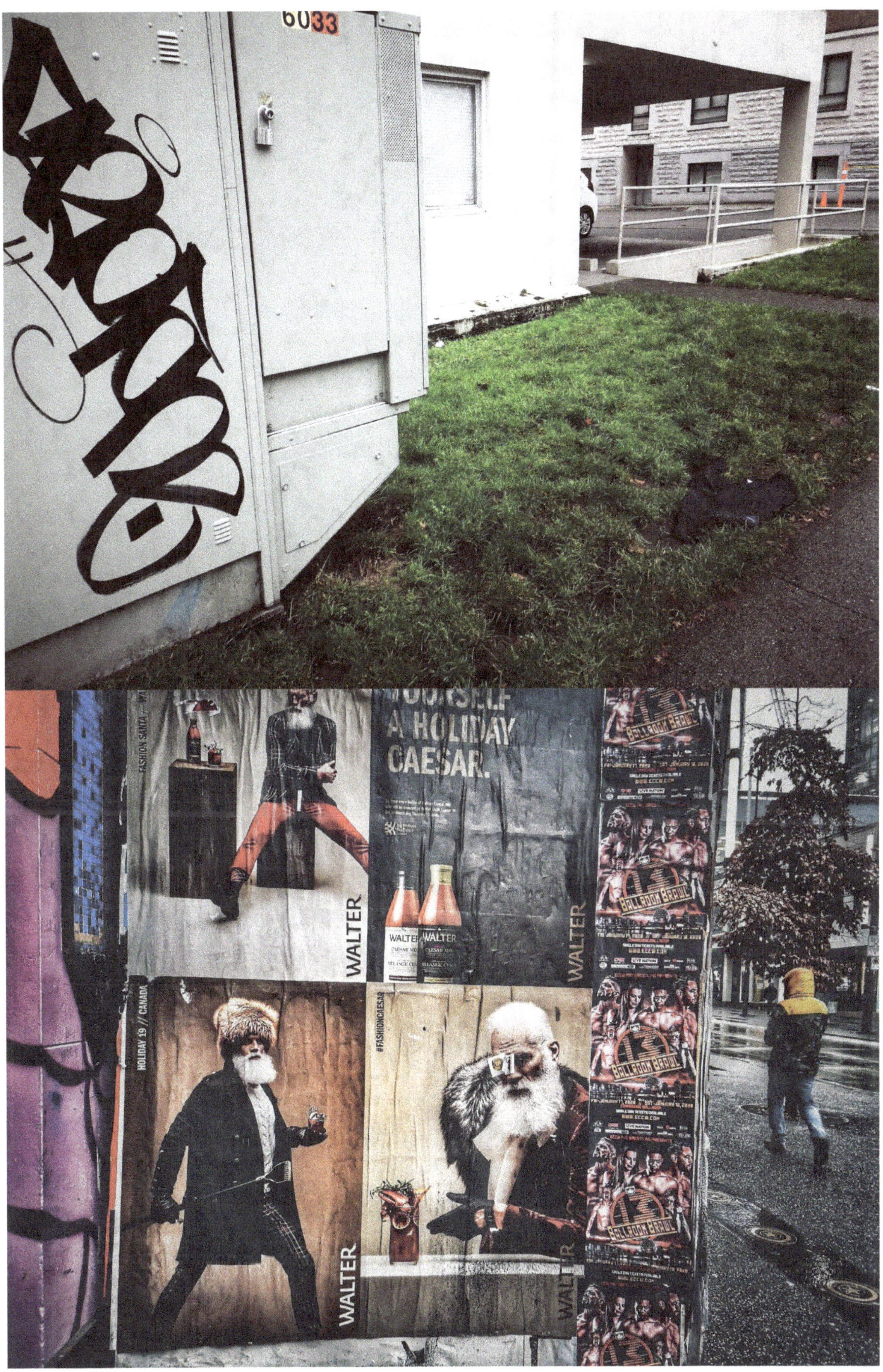
6033
FASHION SANTA
A HOLIDAY CAESAR.
WALTER
WALTER
WALTER
HOLIDAY 19 // CANADA
#FASHIONCAESAR
WALTER
WALTER
BALLROOM BRAWL
BALLROOM BRAWL
BALLROOM BRAWL
BALLROOM BRAWL

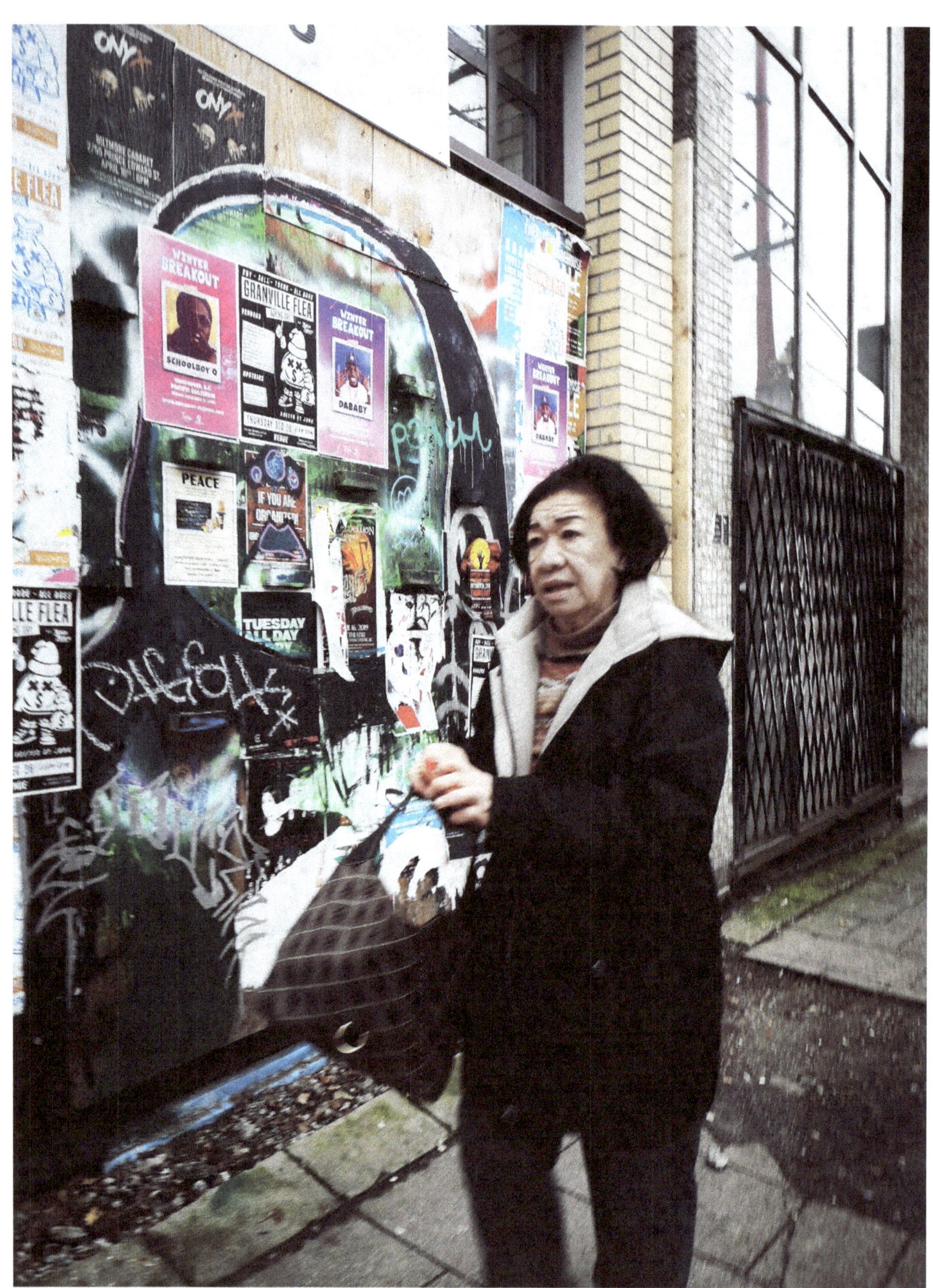

ONYX
ONYX
BILTMORE CABARET
WINTER
BREAKOUT
SCHOOLBOY Q
GRANVILLE FLEA
WINTER
BREAKOUT
DABABY
PEACE
IF YOU ARE
TUESDAY
ALL DAY
DAGFOU
WINTER
BREAKOUT
DABABY
VILLE FLEA

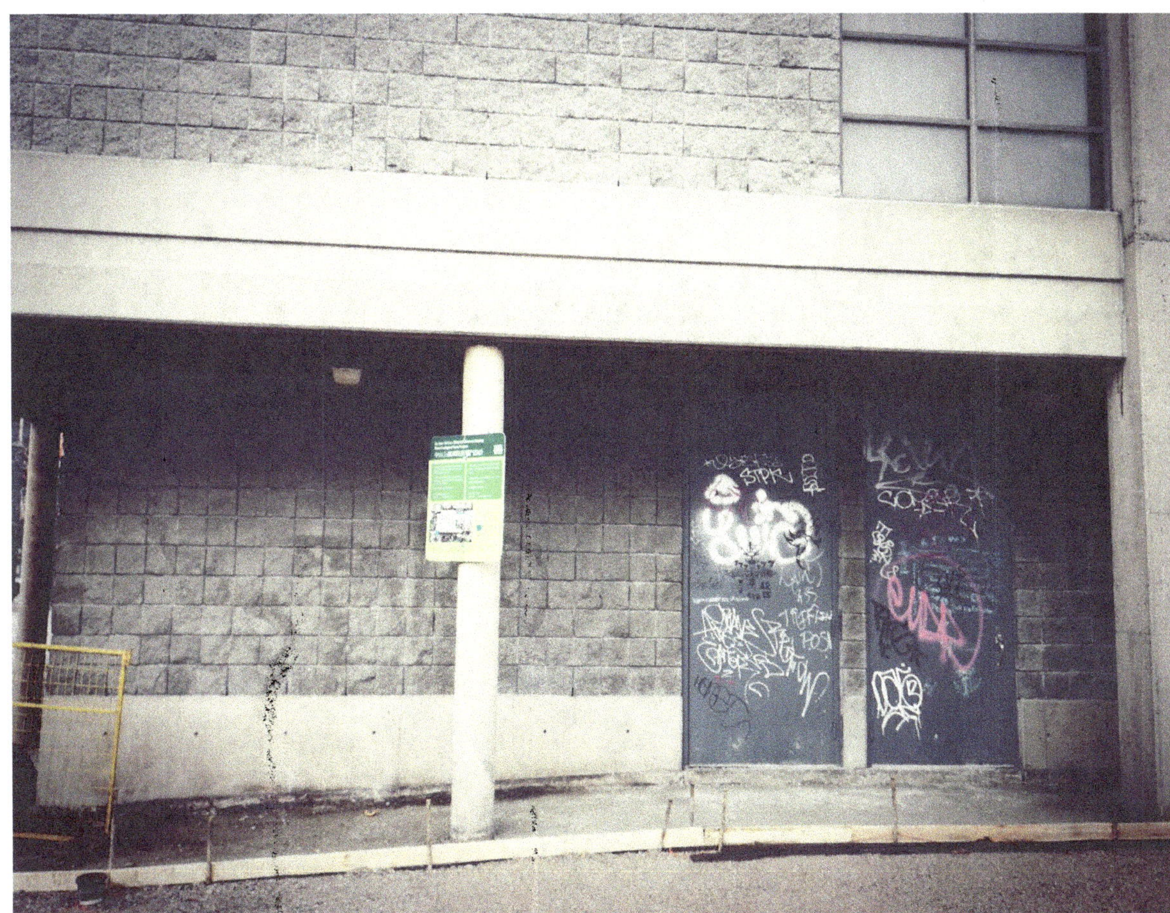
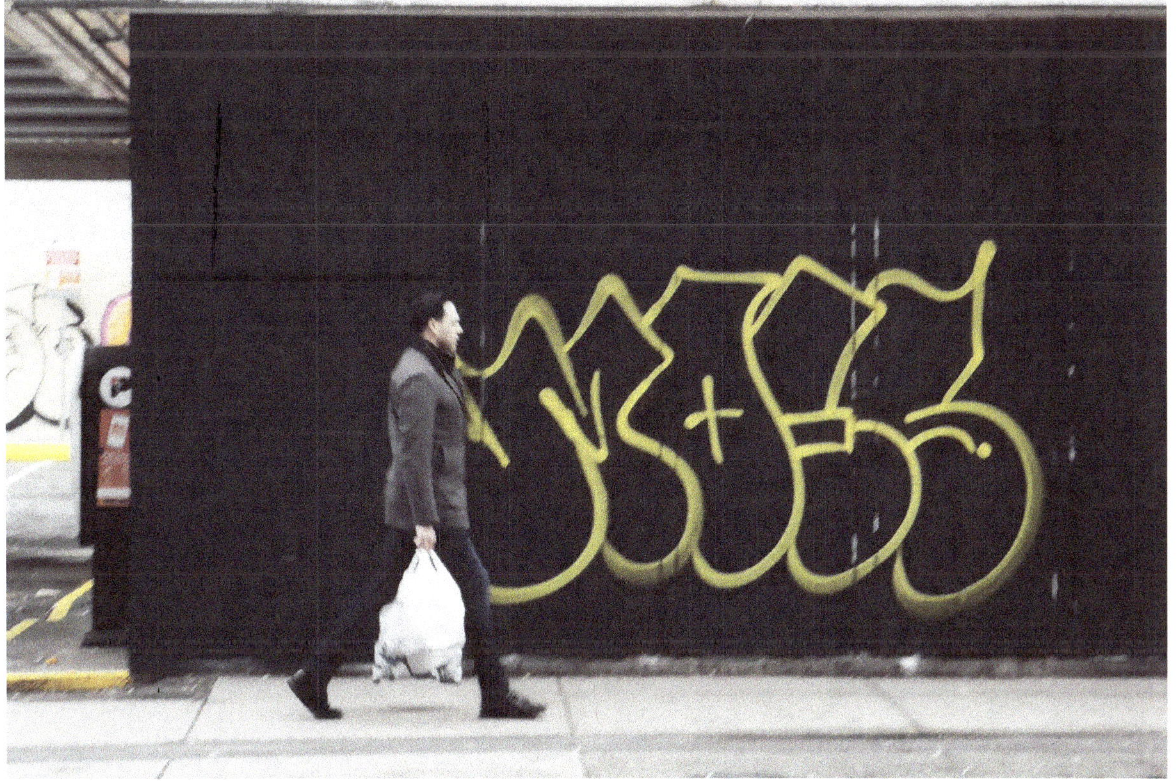
SKY MART Convenience Store
SKY MART
Con

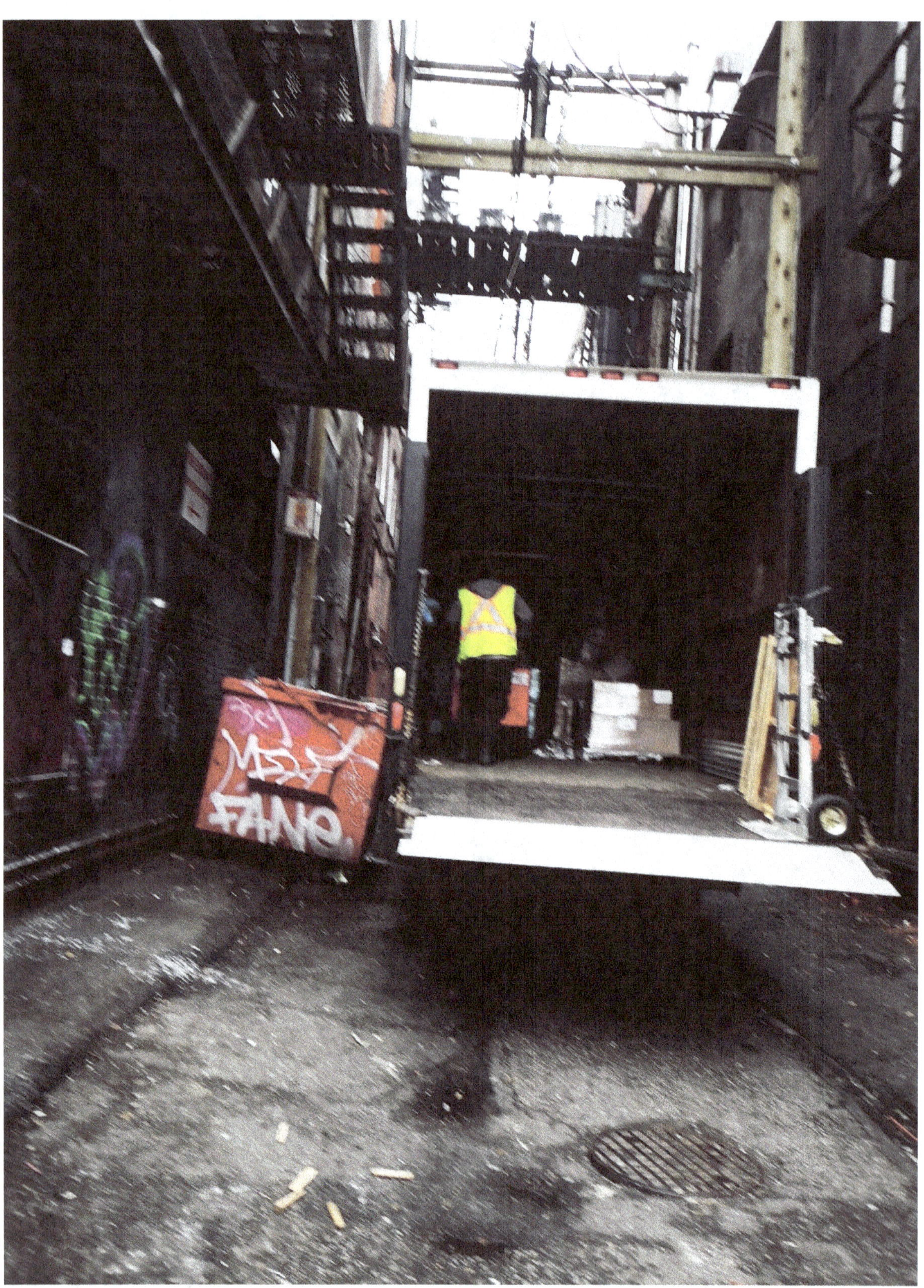

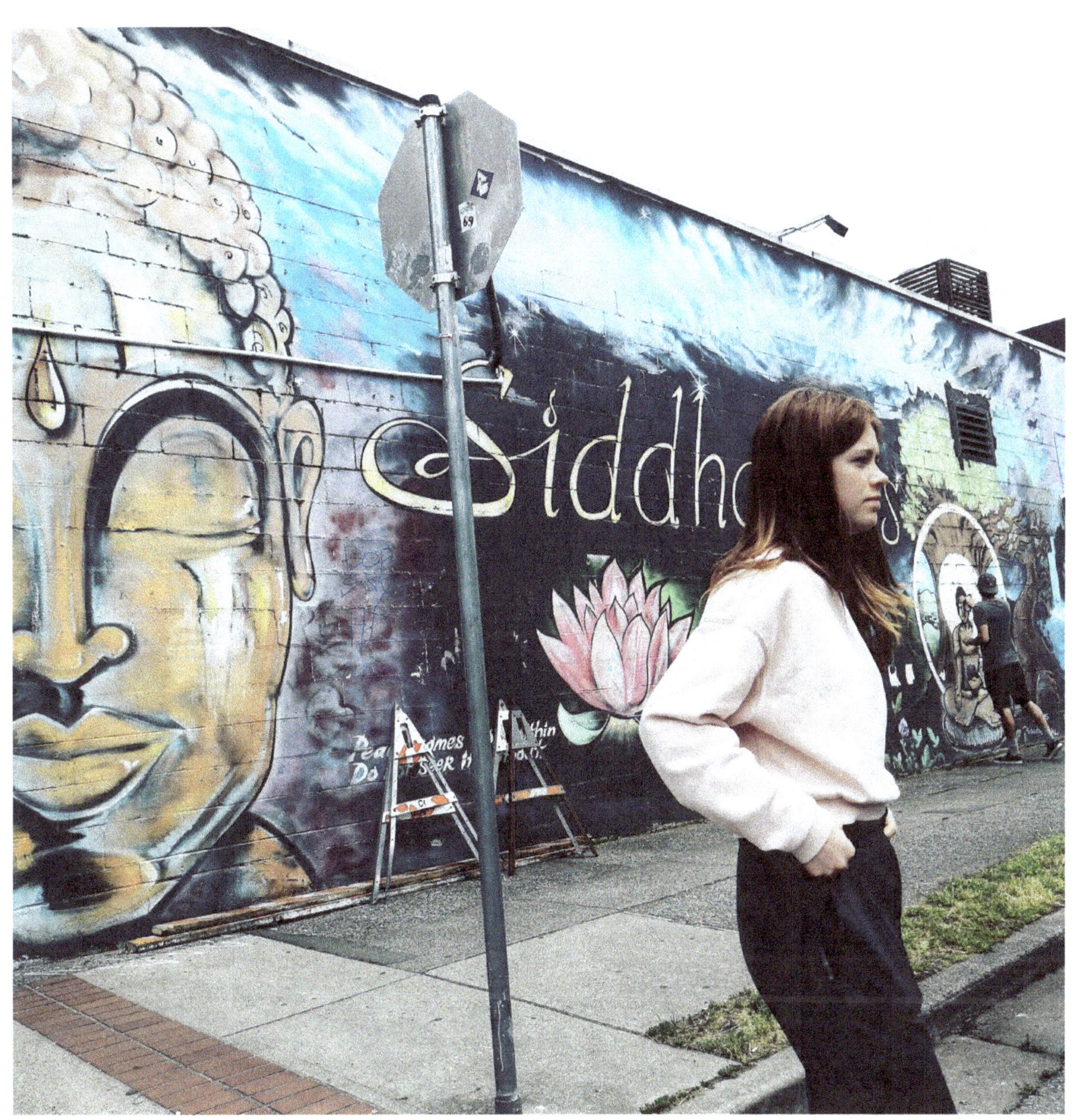
Siddha
Peace comes within
Do not seek it

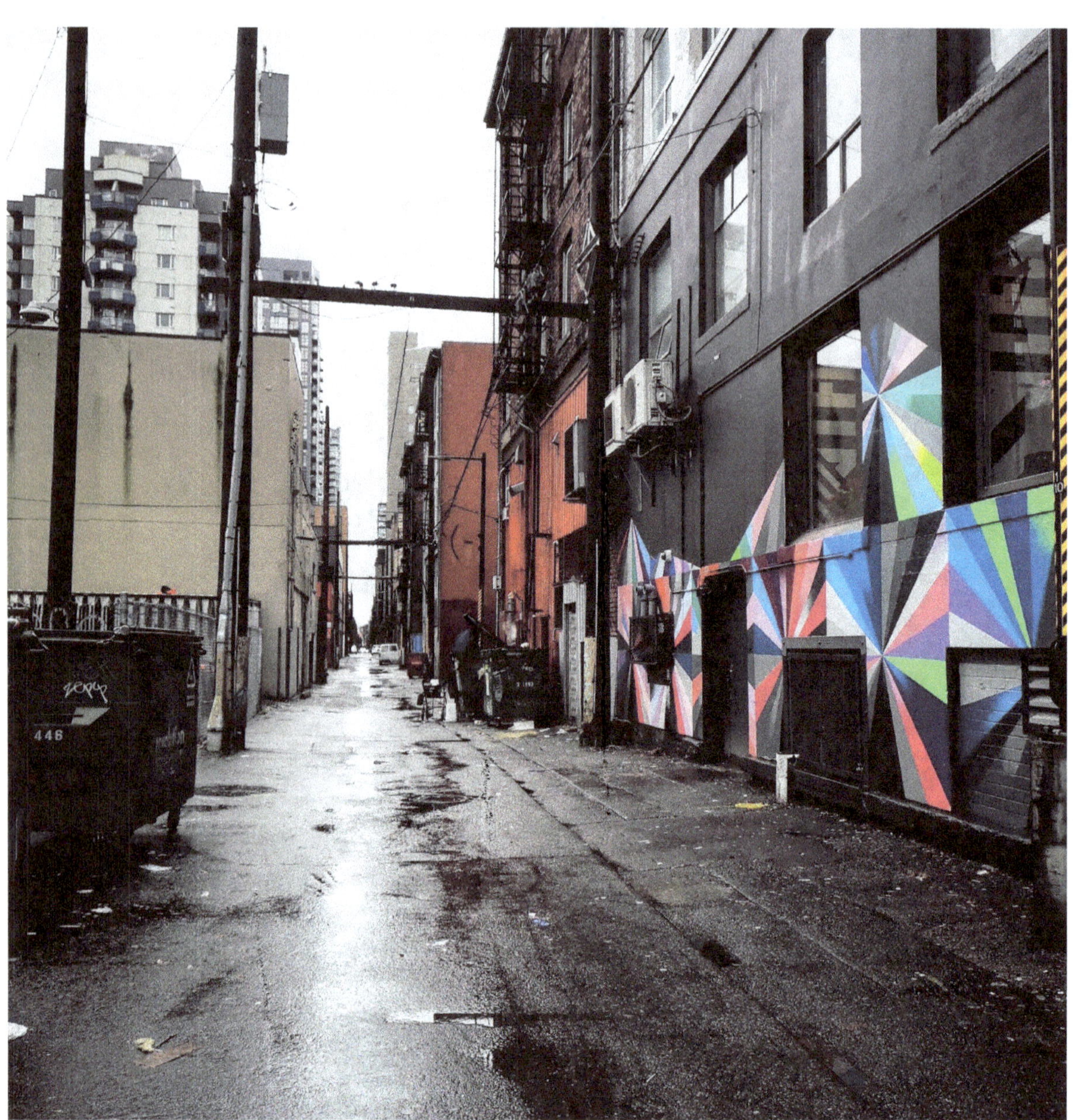

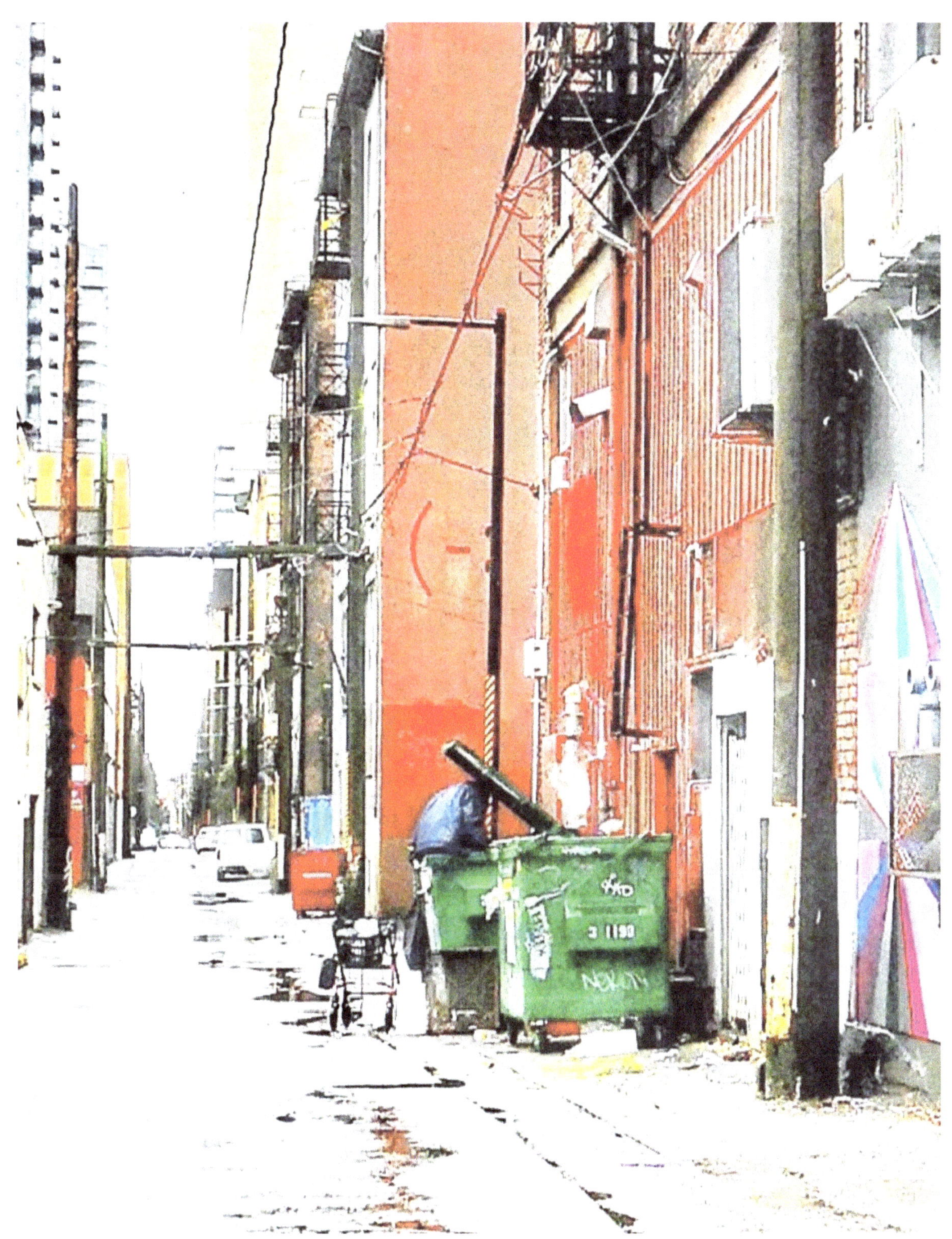

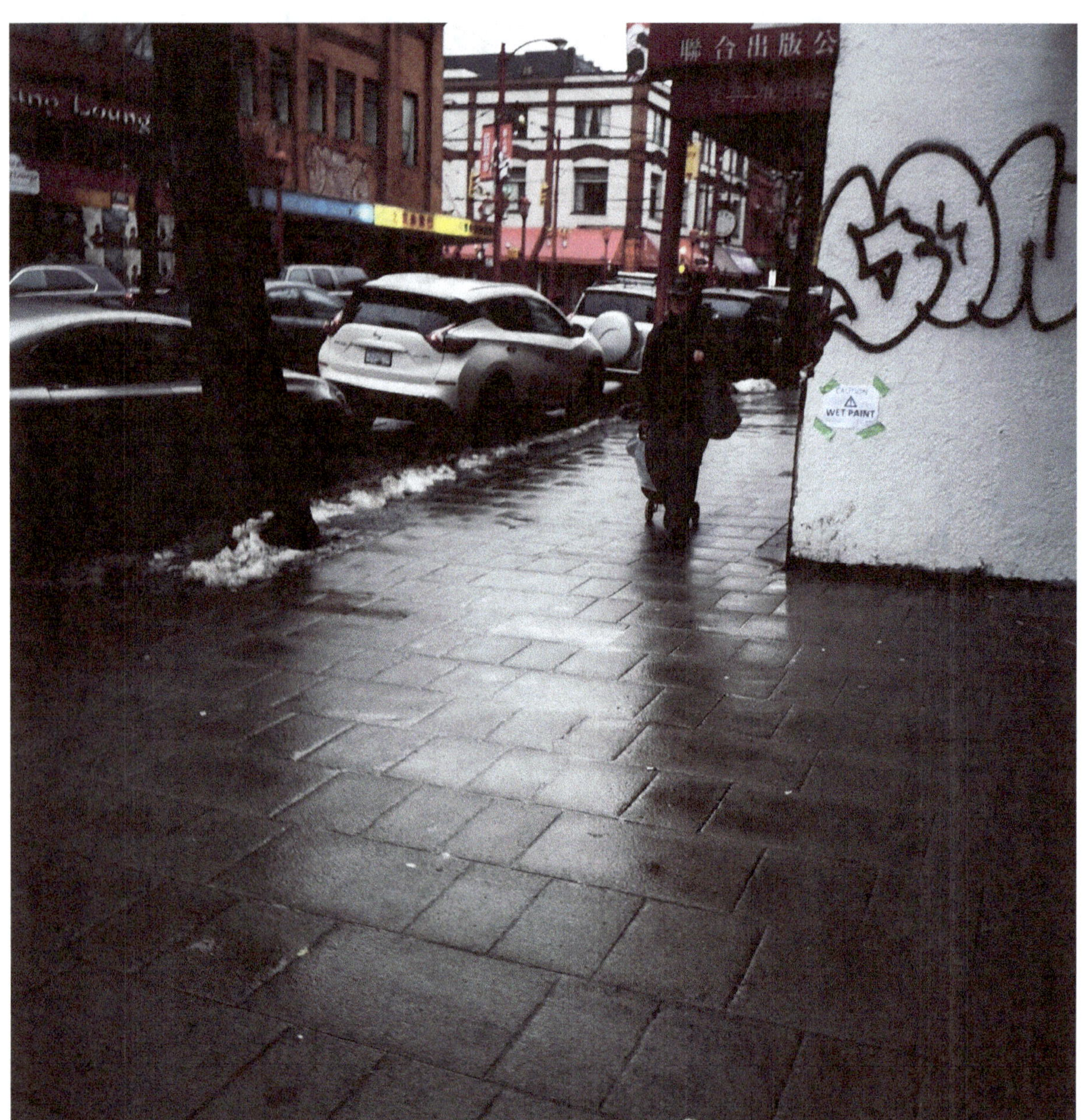
聯合出版公
CAUTION
WET PAINT

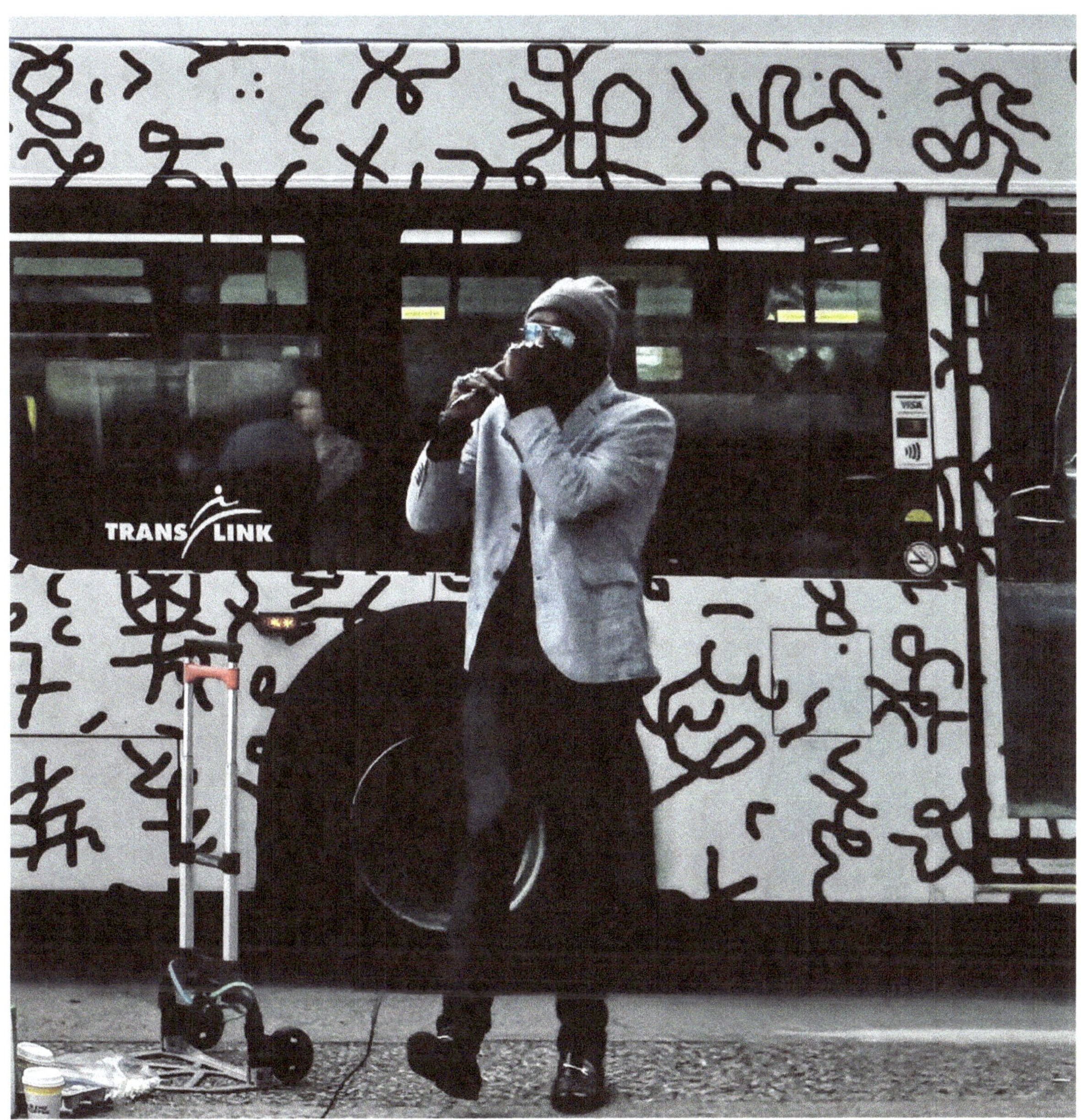

TRANS LINK
VISA

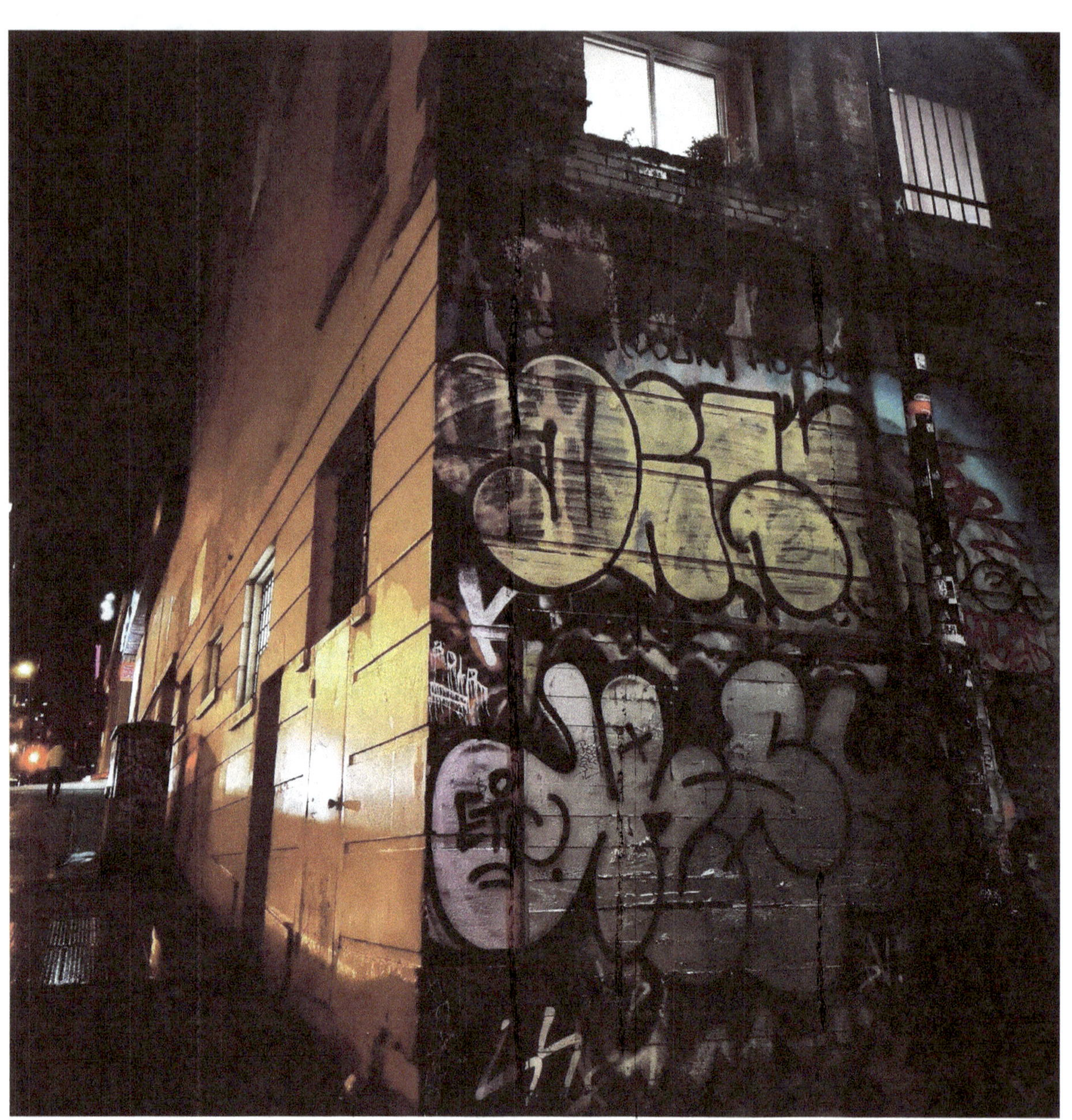

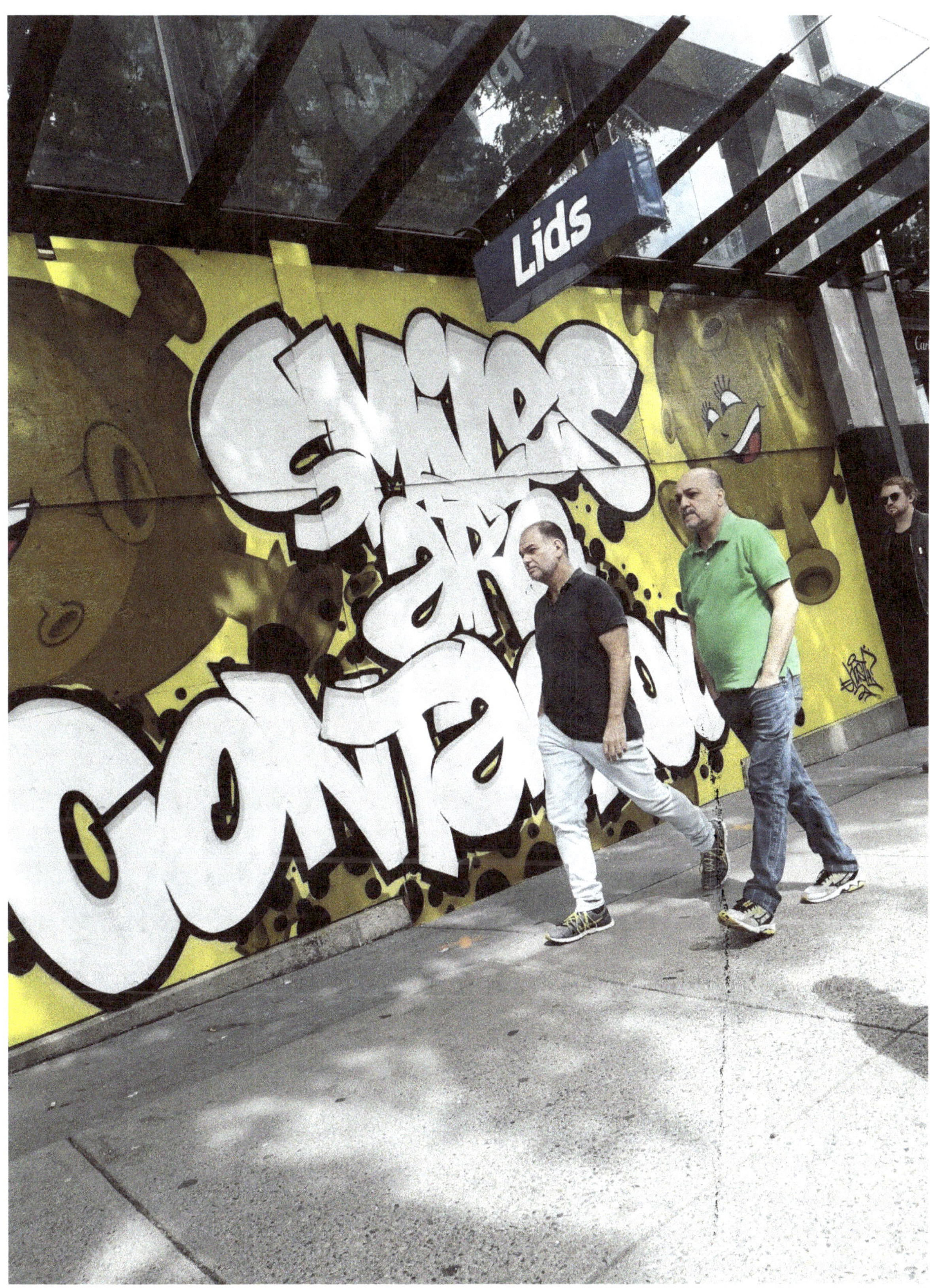

Lids
SMILES
ARE
CONTAGIOUS

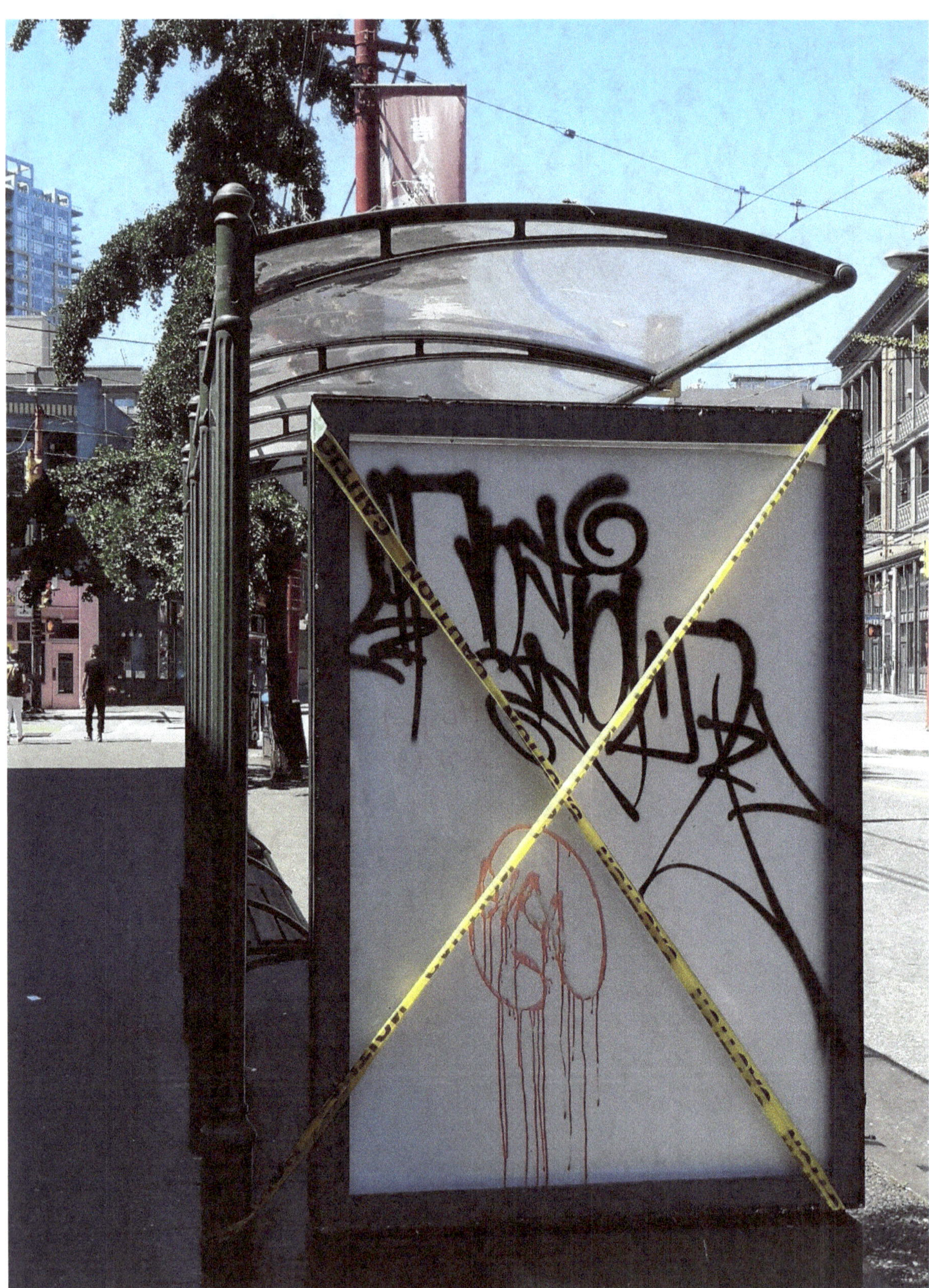

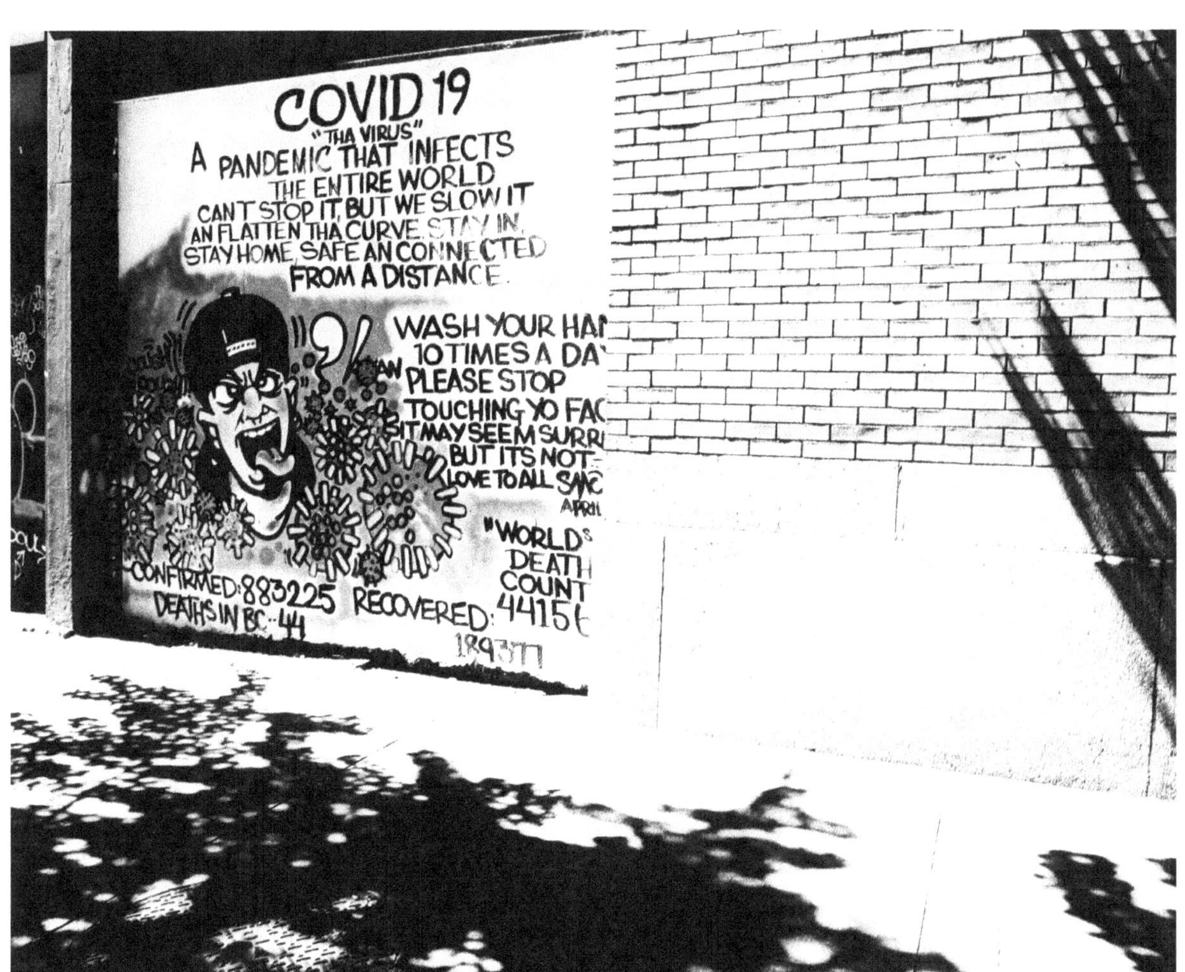

COVID 19
"THA VIRUS"
A PANDEMIC THAT INFECTS
THE ENTIRE WORLD
CAN'T STOP IT, BUT WE SLOW IT
AN FLATTEN THA CURVE. STAY IN,
STAY HOME, SAFE AN CONNECTED
FROM A DISTANCE.
WASH YOUR HAN
10 TIMES A DA
AN PLEASE STOP
TOUCHING YO FAC
IT MAY SEEM SURR
BUT ITS NOT
LOVE TO ALL SNC
APRIL
"WORLD'S
DEATH
COUNT
CONFIRMED: 883225 RECOVERED: 44156
DEATHS IN BC : 44
189377

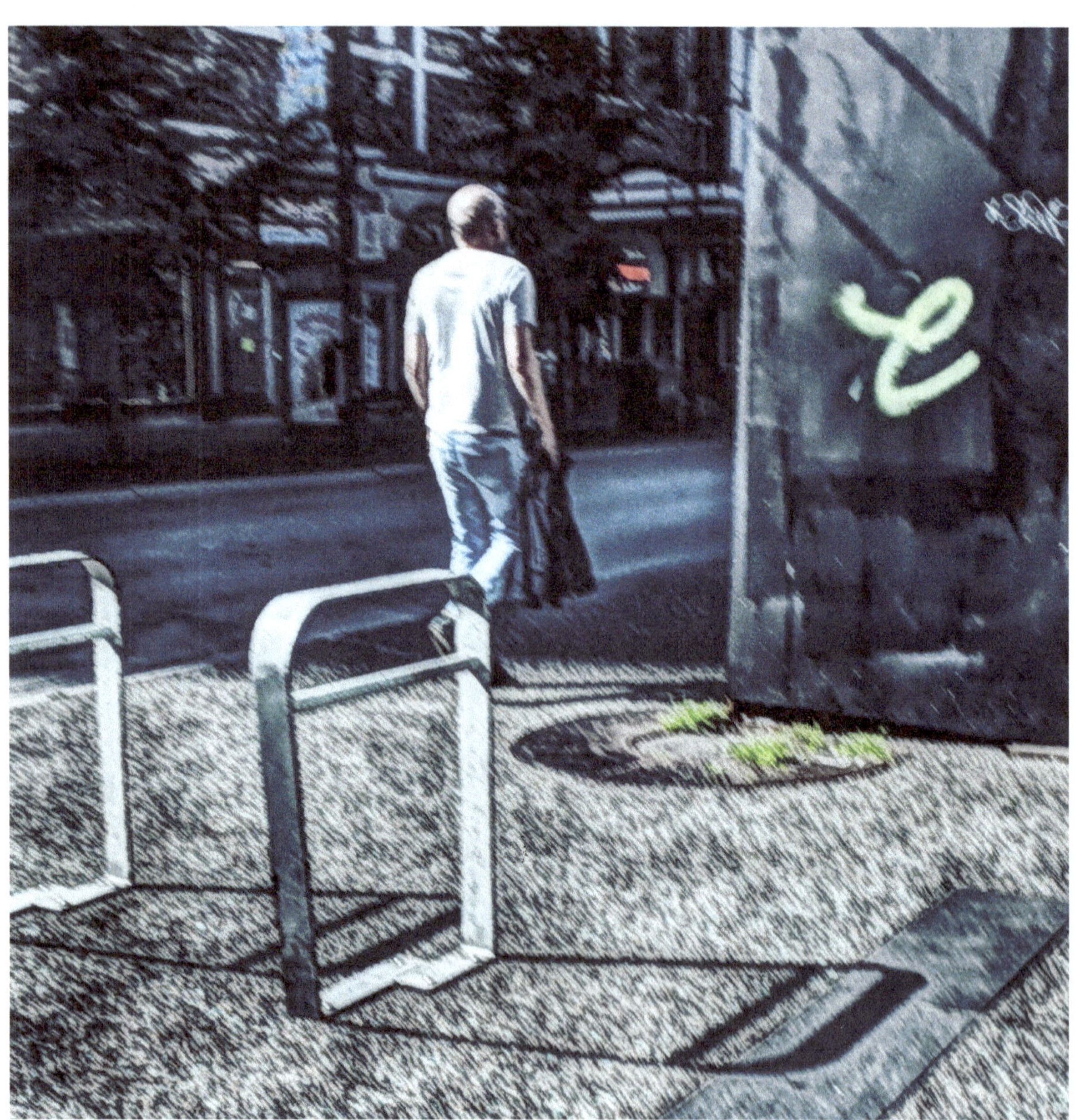

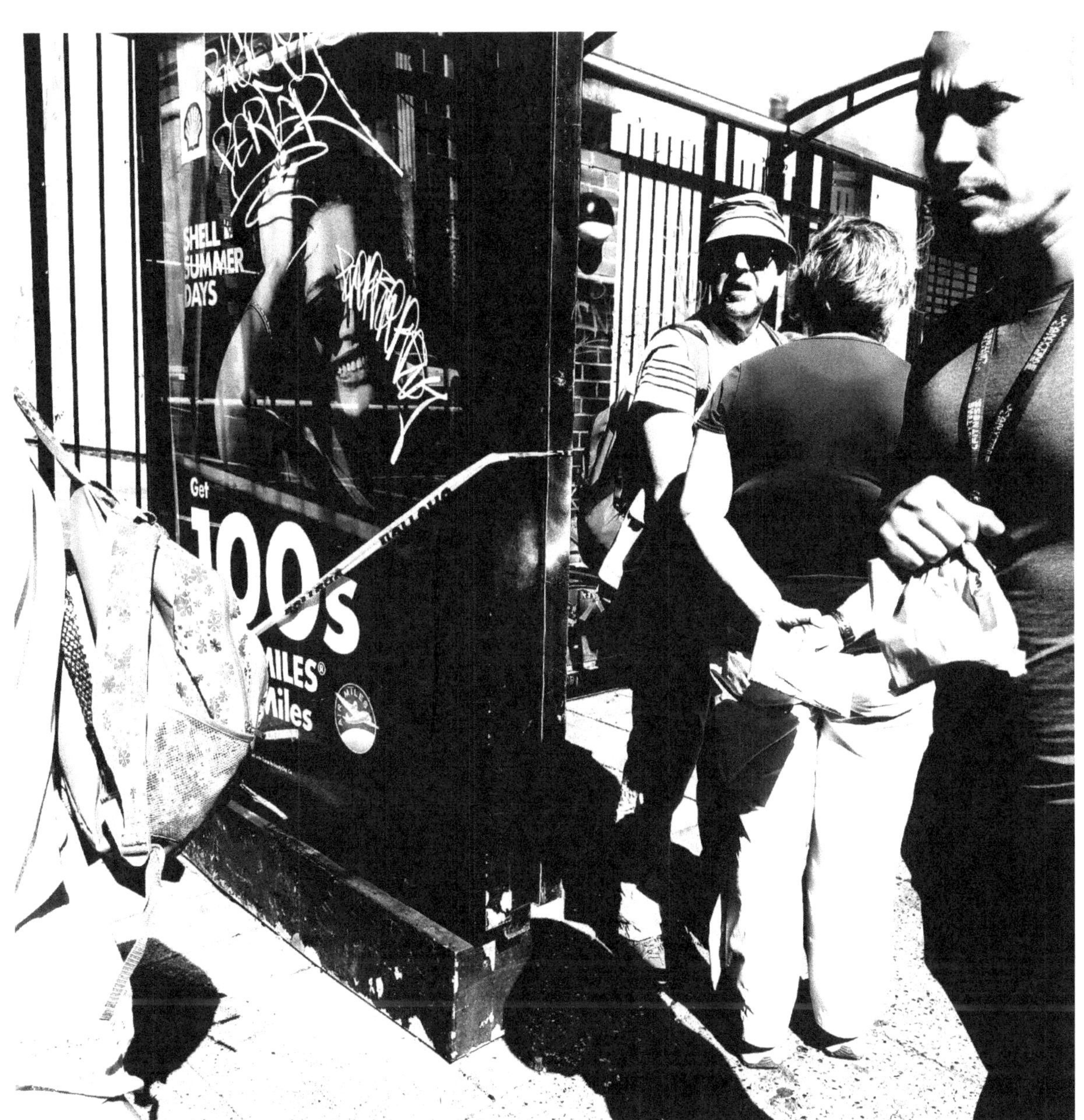

SHELL
SHELL
SUMMER
DAYS
Get
100s
MILES®
Miles
AIR MILES

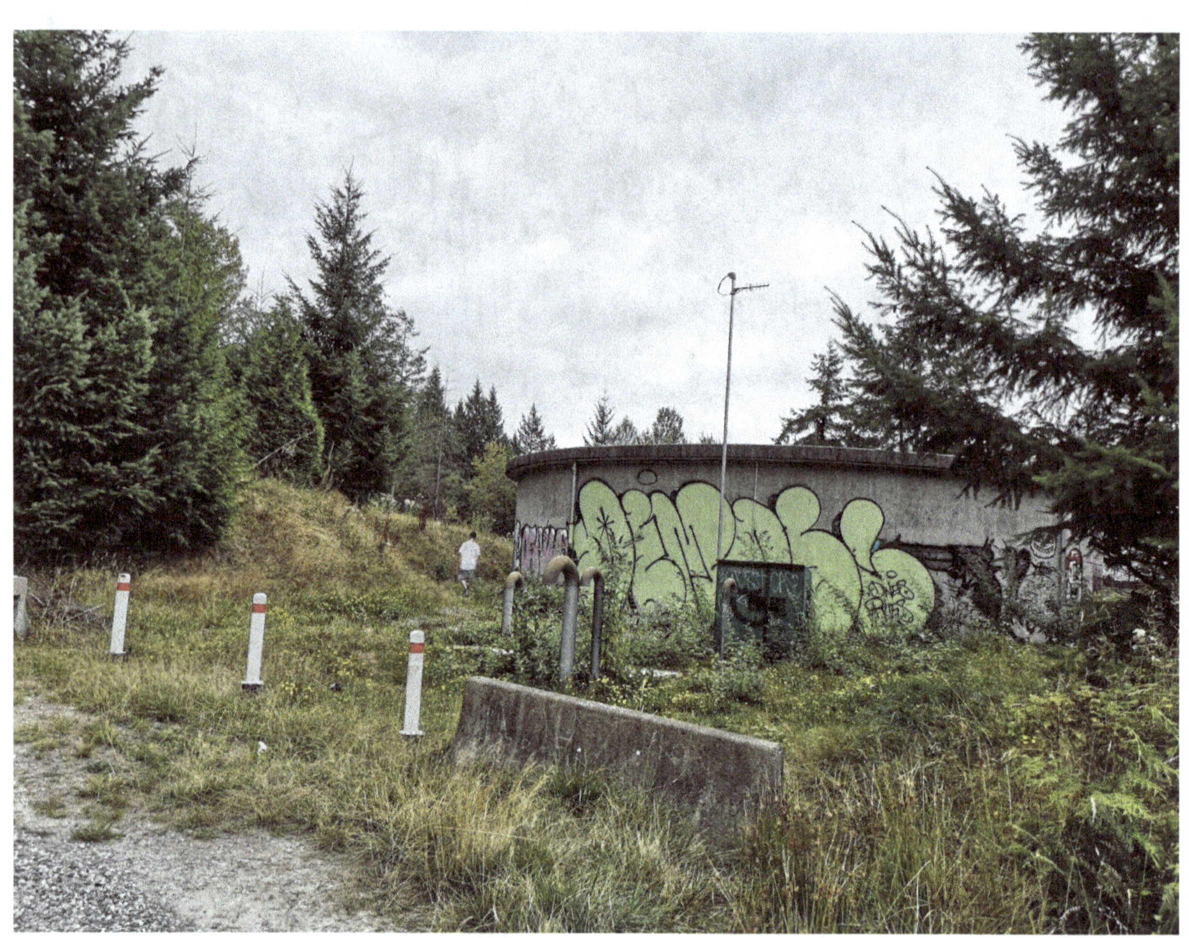

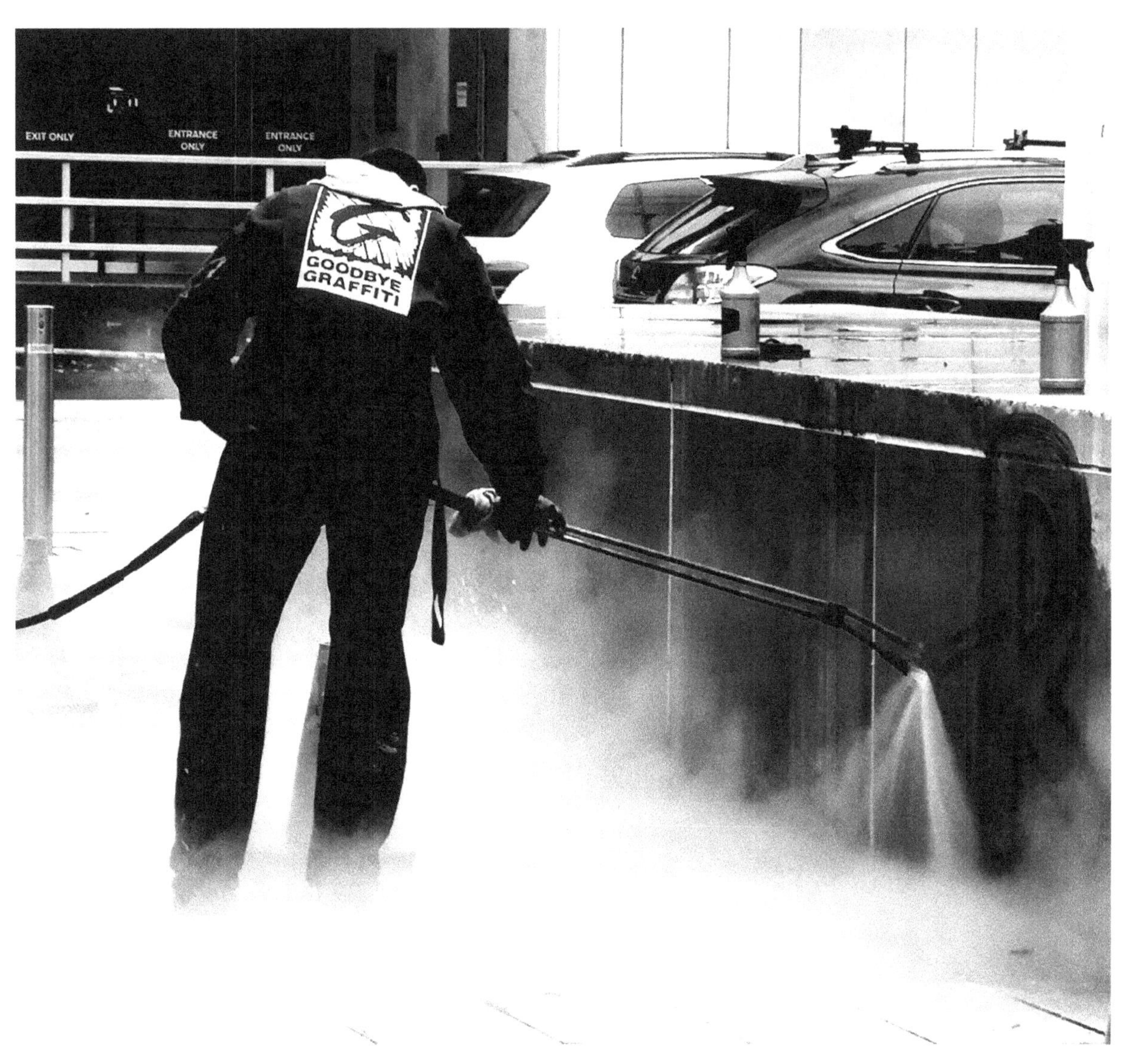

EXIT ONLY
ENTRANCE ONLY
ENTRANCE ONLY
GOODBYE GRAFFITI

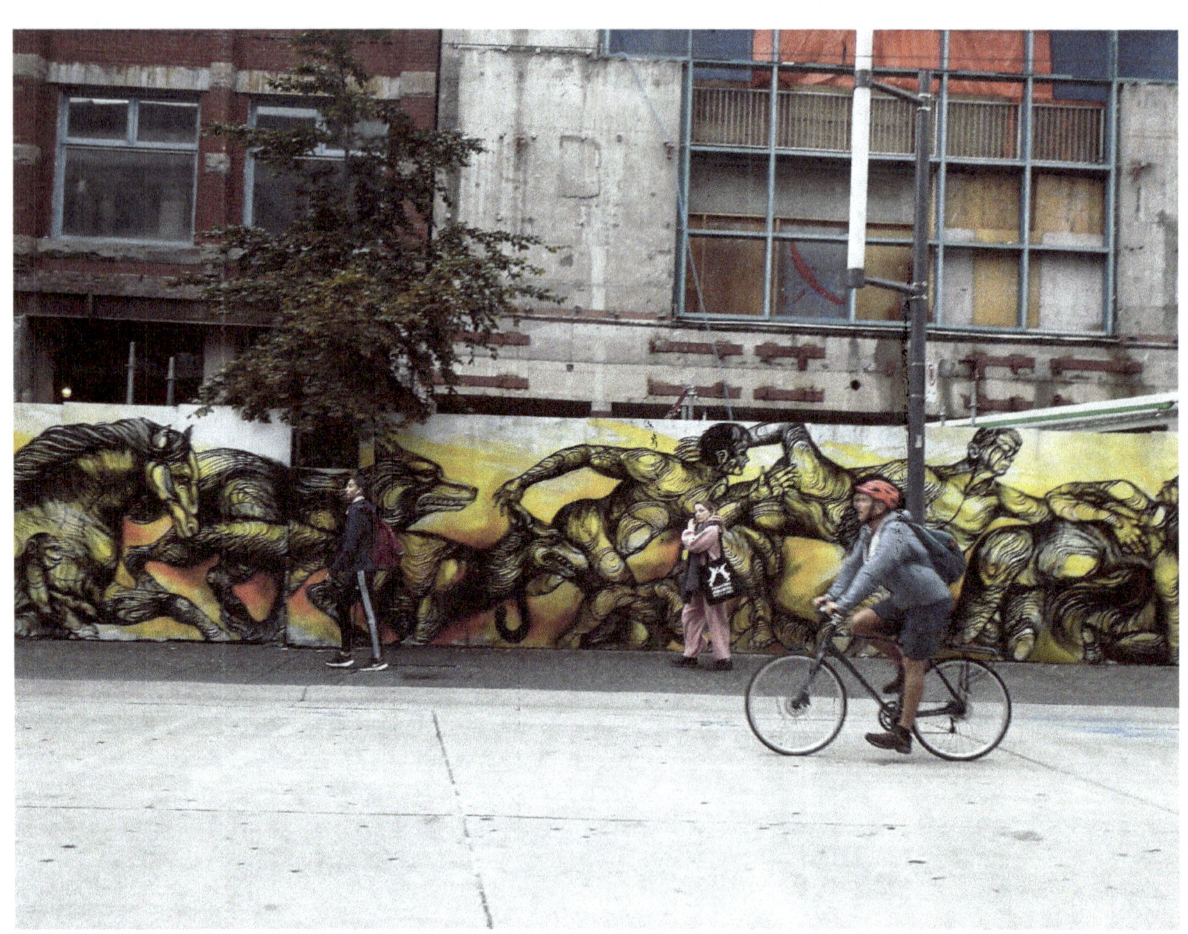

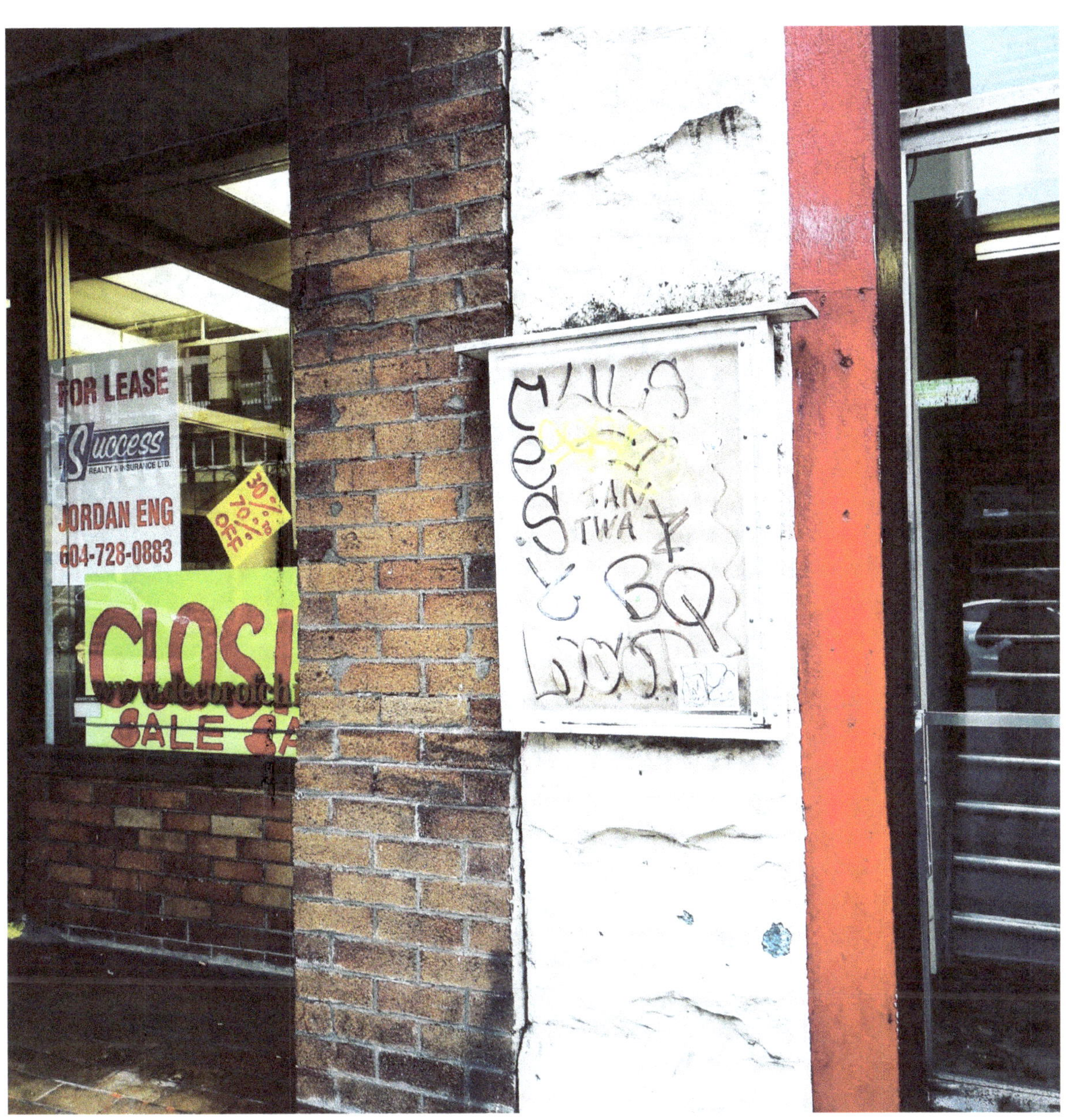
FOR LEASE
Success
REALTY & INSURANCE LTD.
JORDAN ENG
604-728-0883
30% 50% 70% OFF
CLOS
SALE

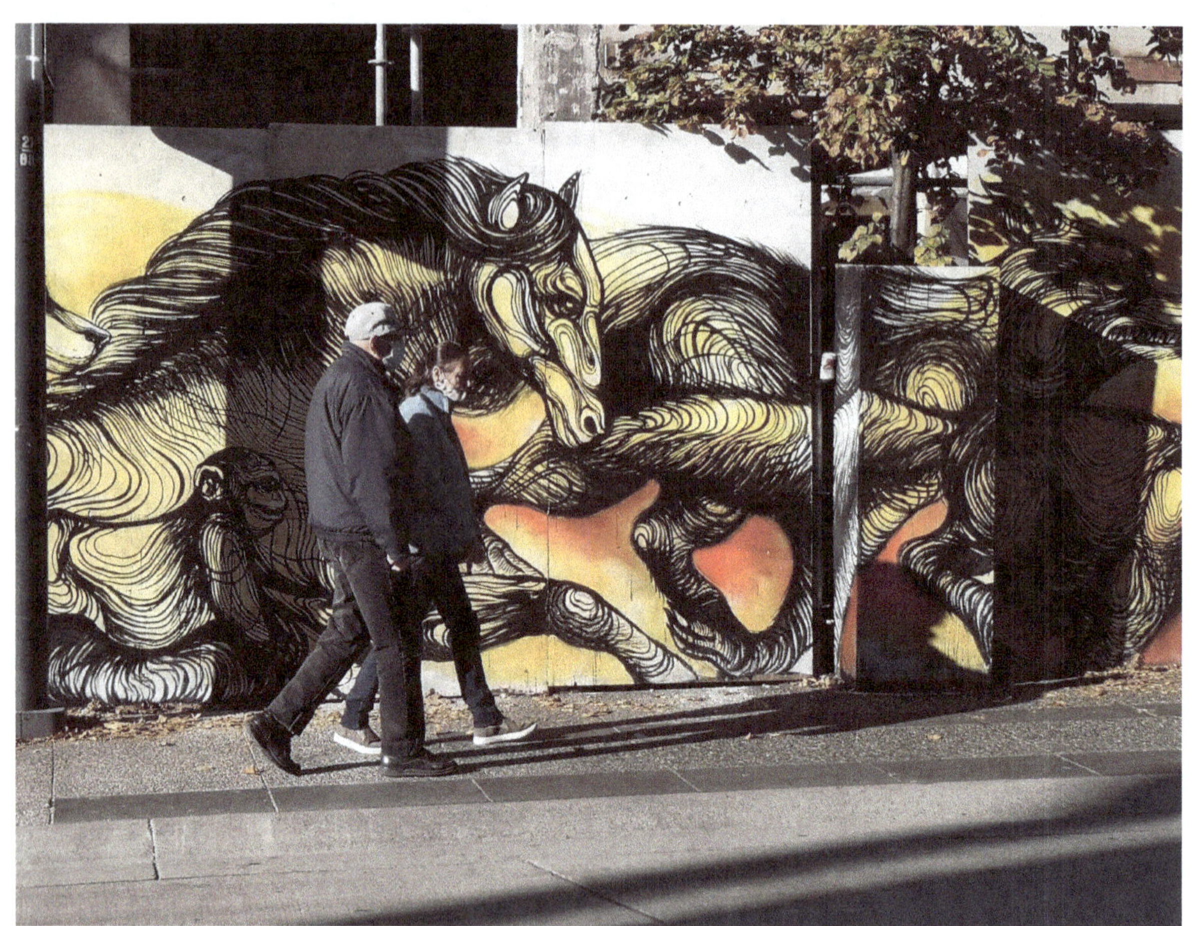

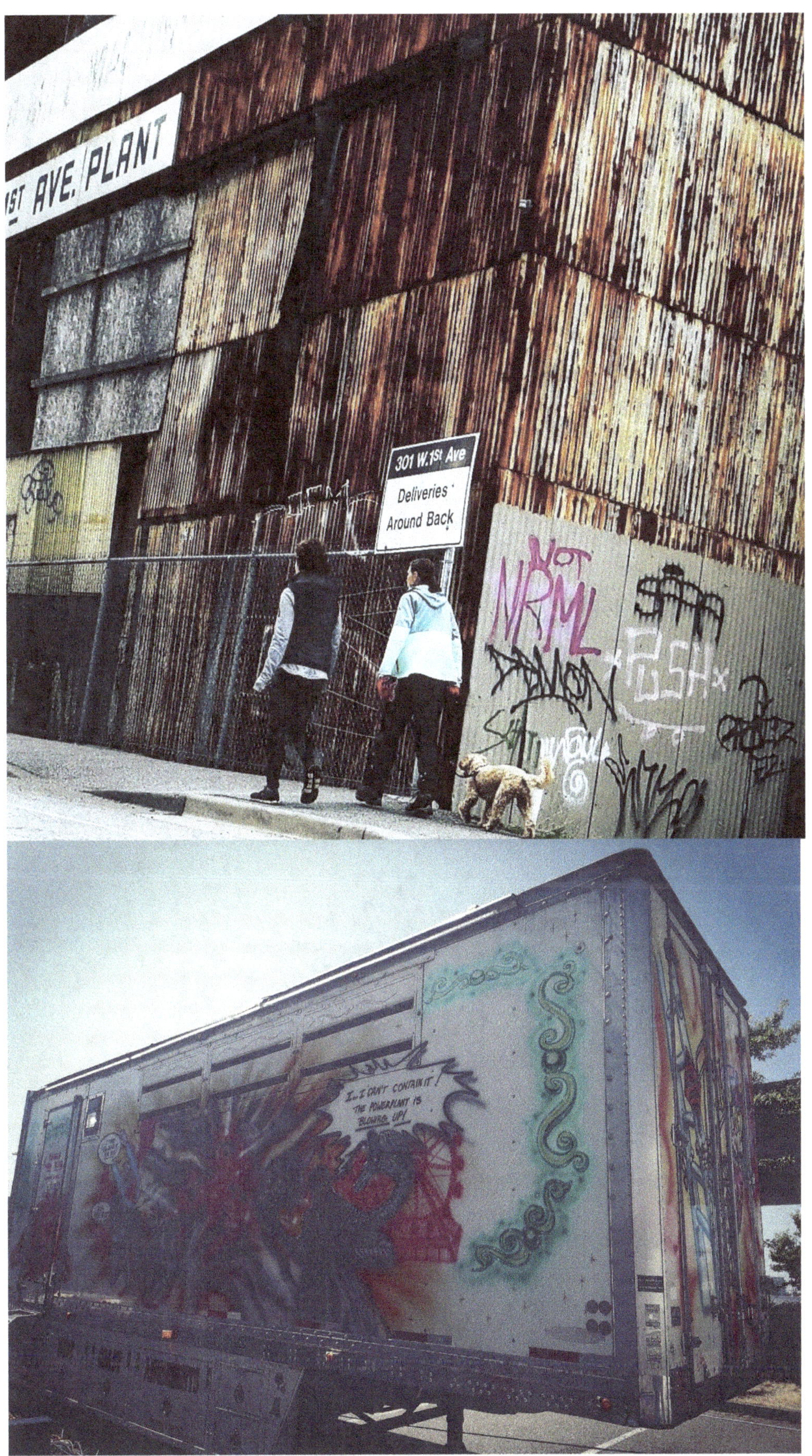
1st AVE. PLANT
301 W. 1st Ave
Deliveries
Around Back
NOT
NRML
DEMON
PUSH
I... I CAN'T CONTAIN IT!
THE POWERPLANT IS
BLOWING UP!

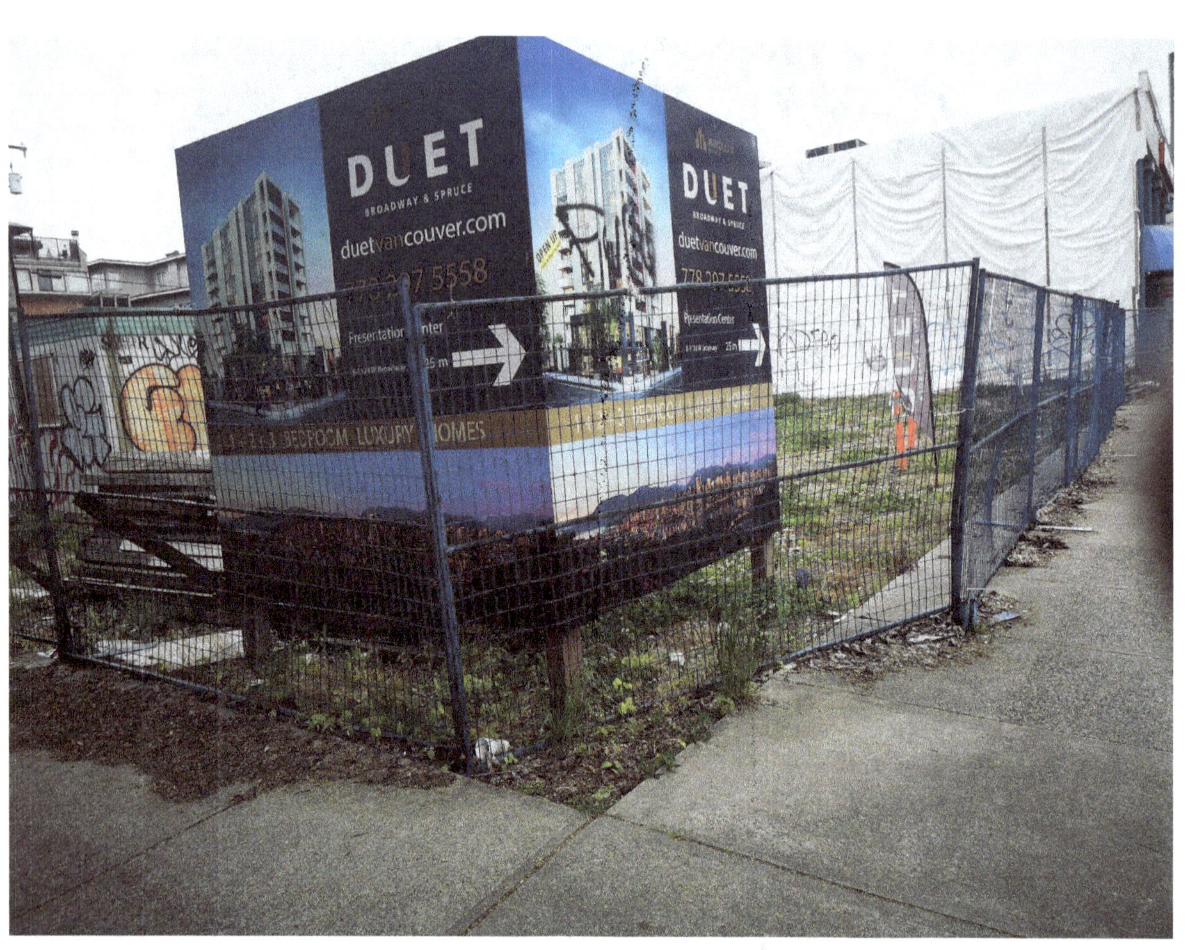
DUET
BROADWAY & SPRUCE
duetvancouver.com
778 207 5558
Presentation Center
25 m
DUET
BROADWAY & SPRUCE
duetvancouver.com
778 207 5558
Presentation Center
25 m
1 - 2 & 3 BEDROOM LUXURY HOMES

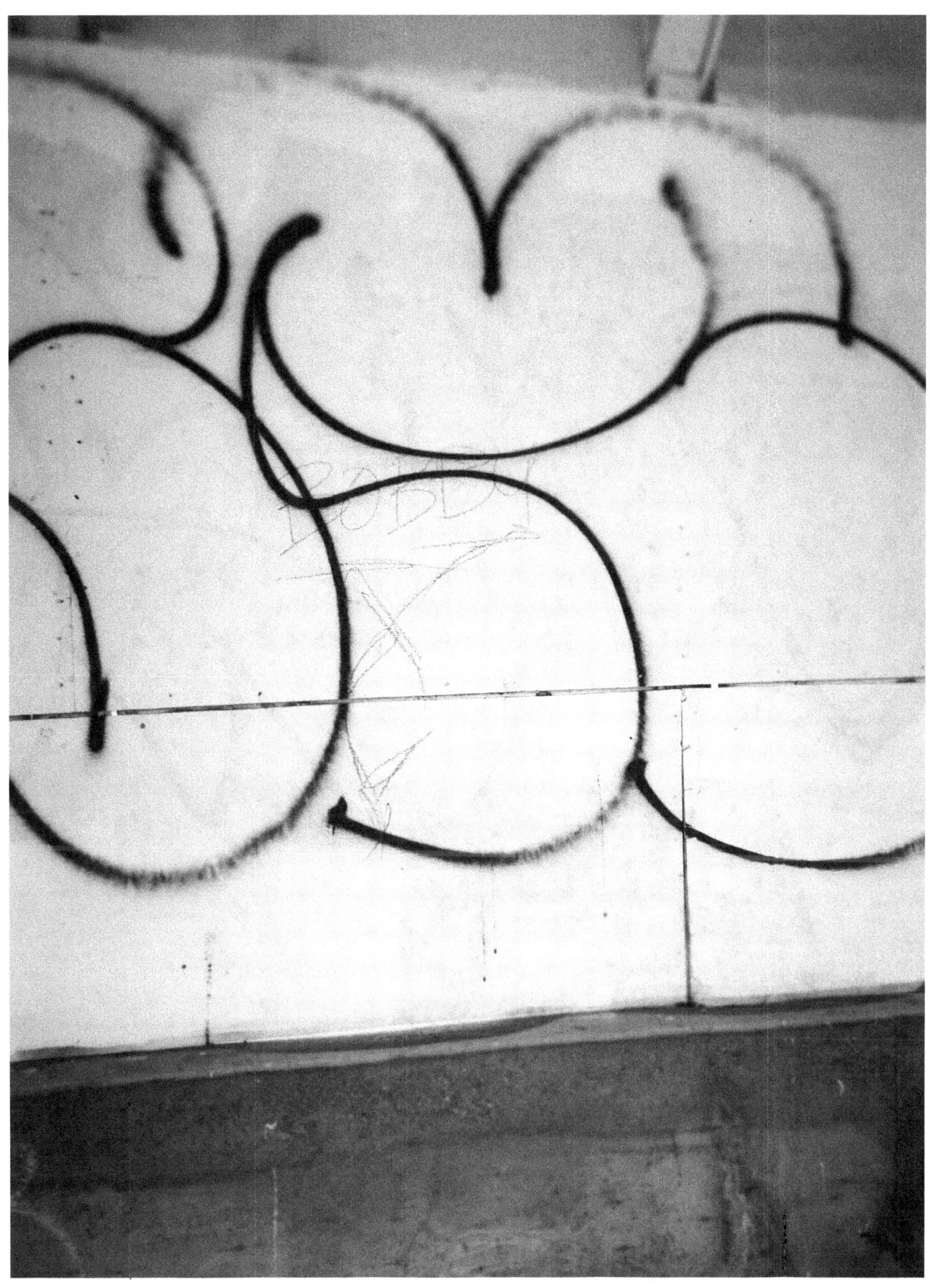

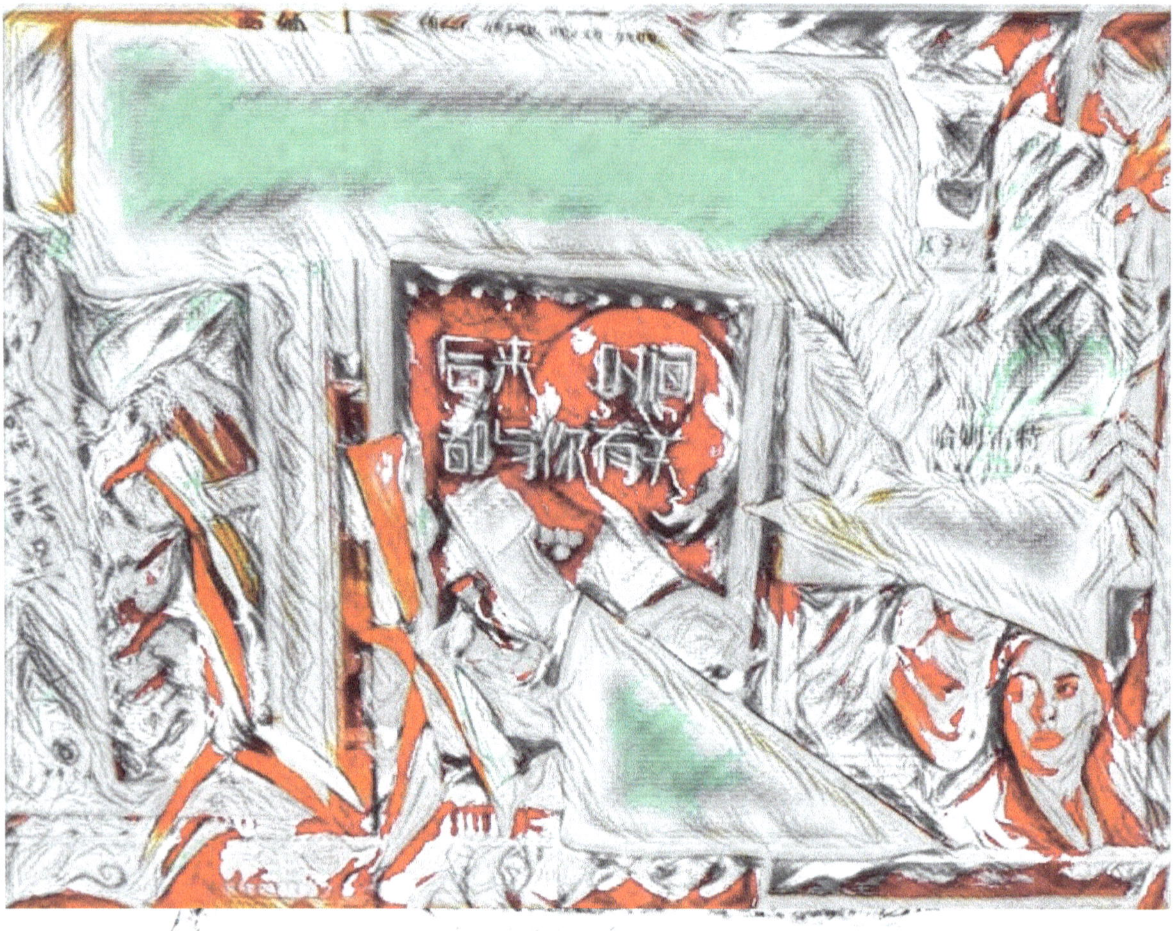

HAPPY HALLOWEEN
TRICK OR TREAT
HAPPY HALLOWEEN ✦ HAPPY HALLO

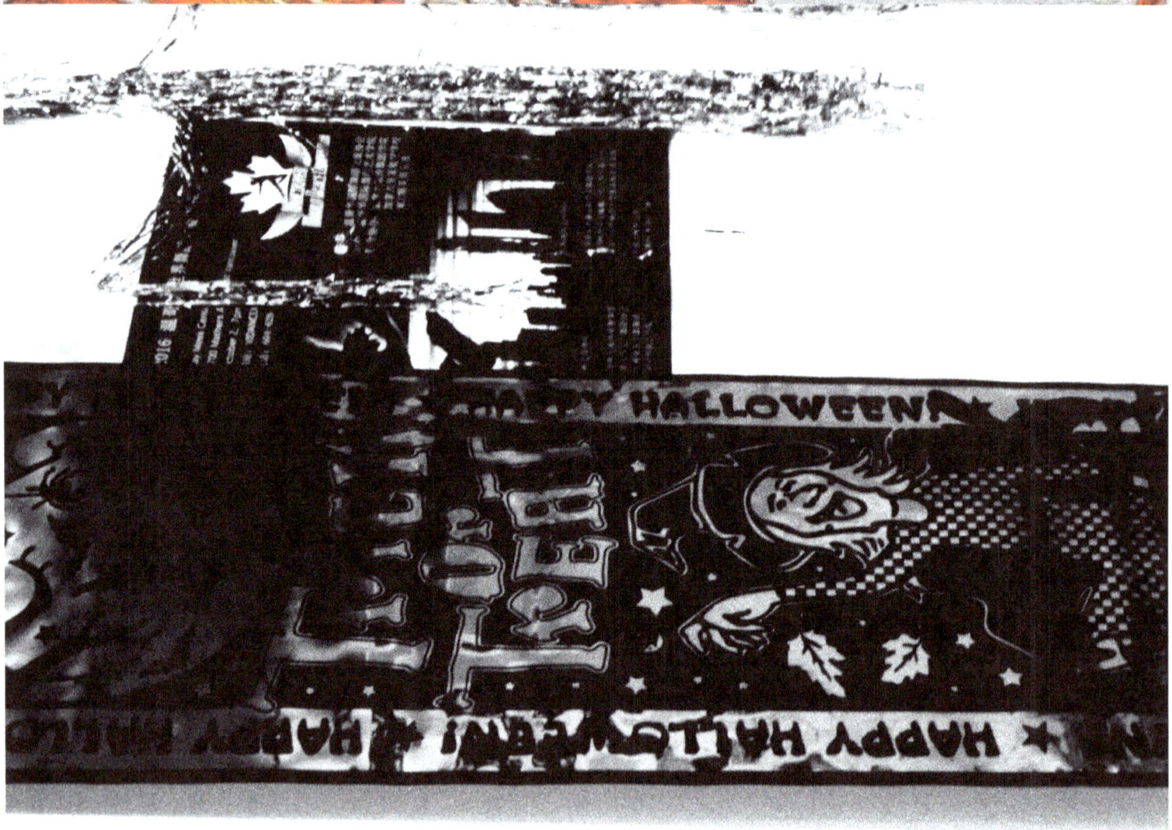

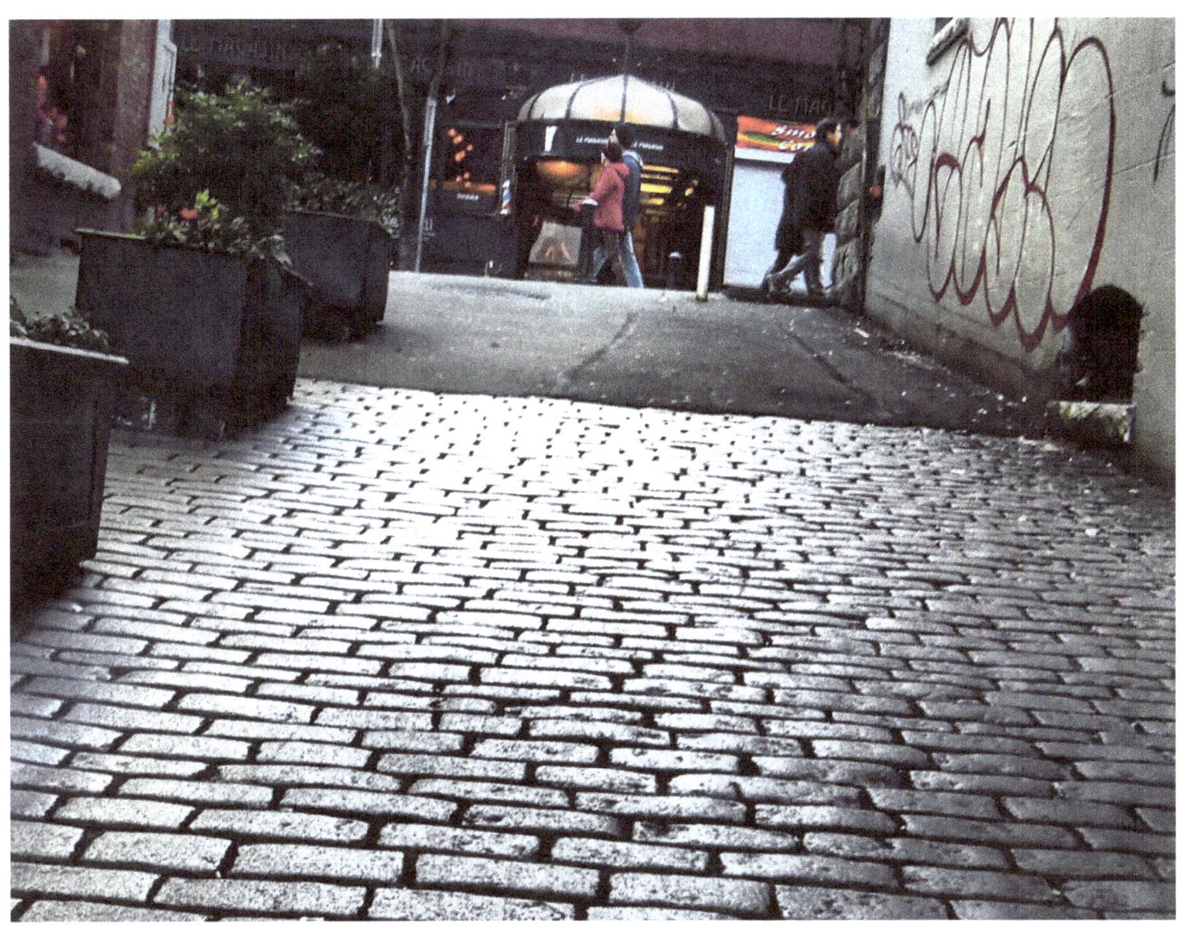

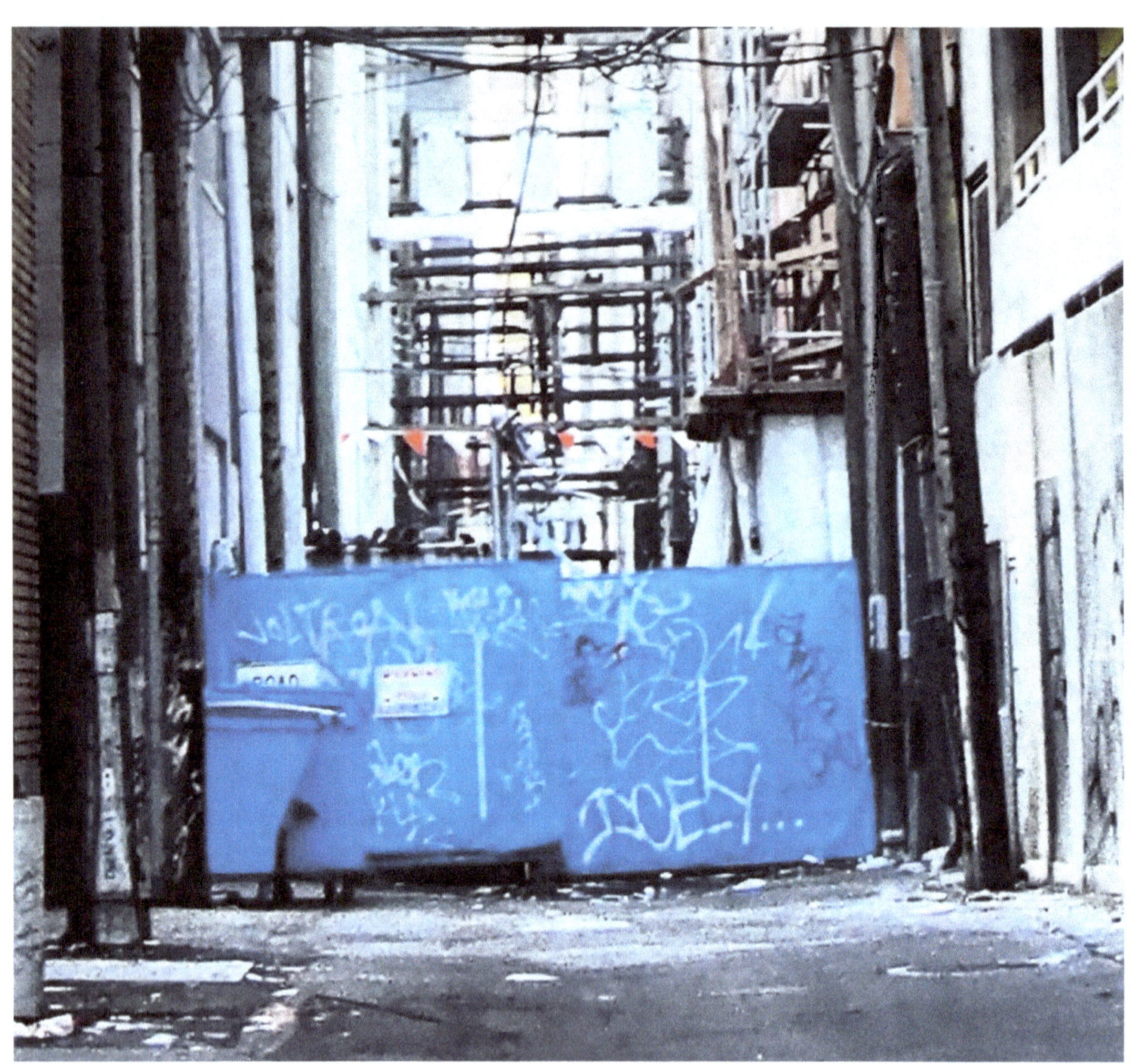
VOLTRON
JOEY...

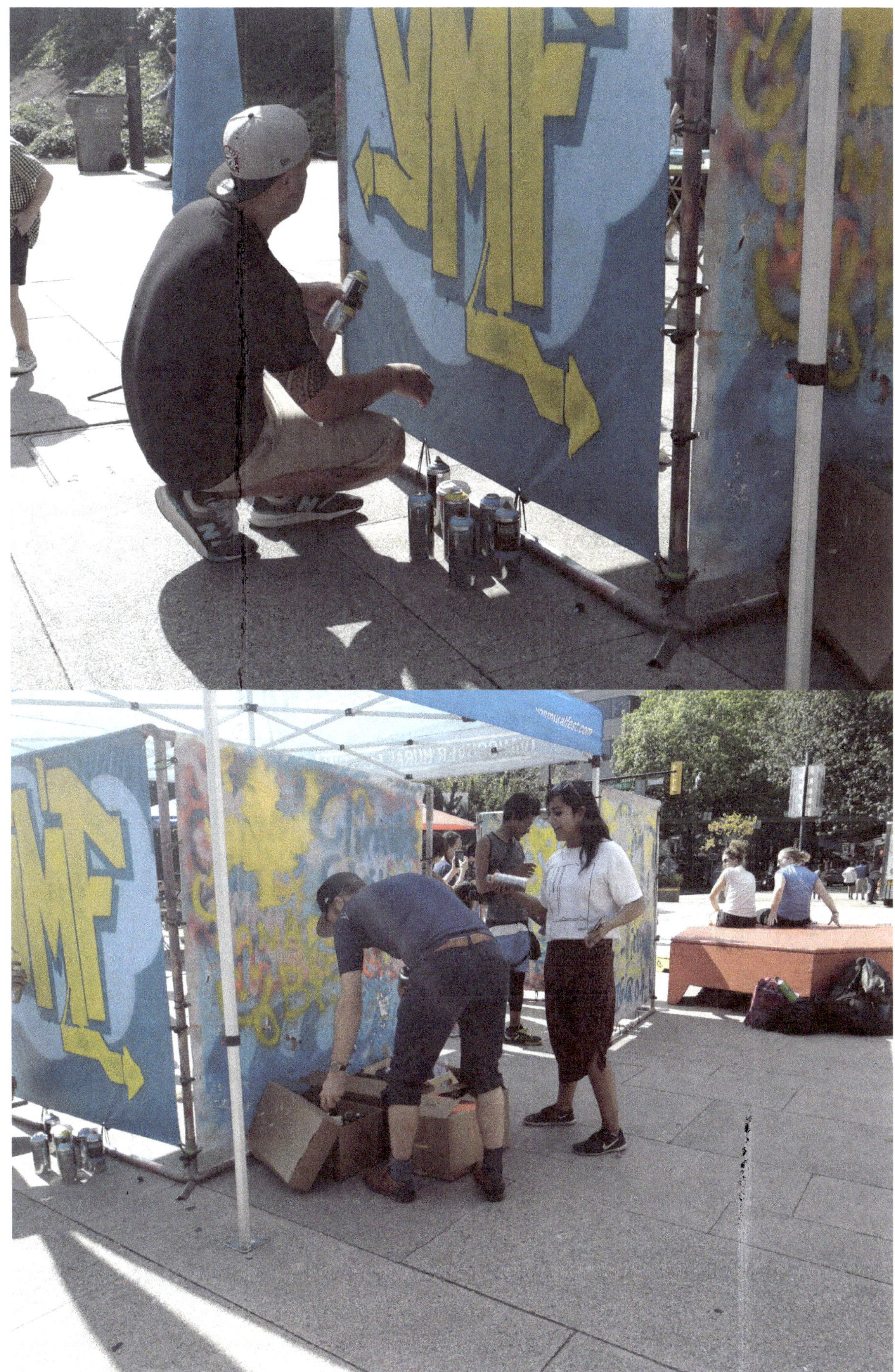

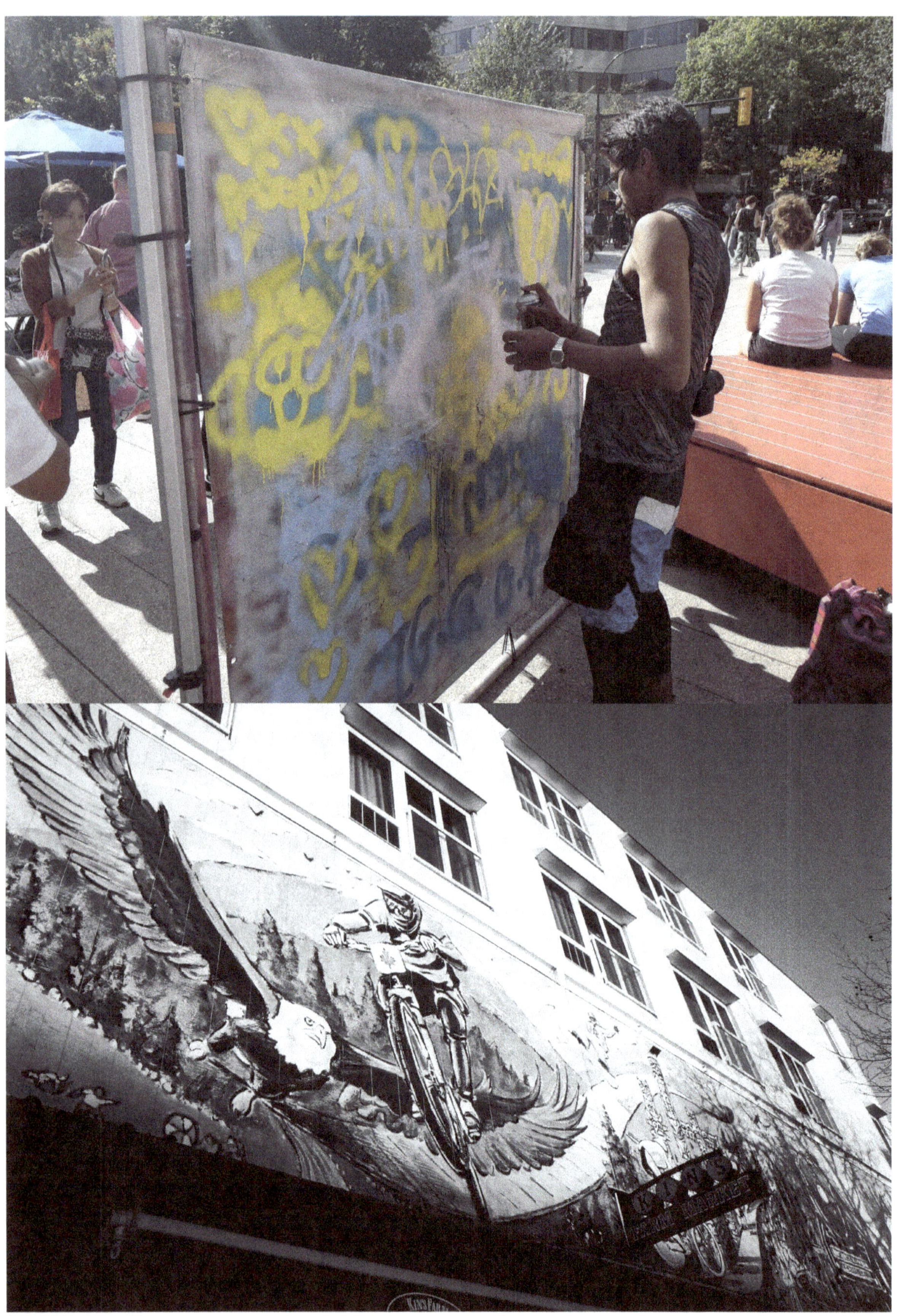

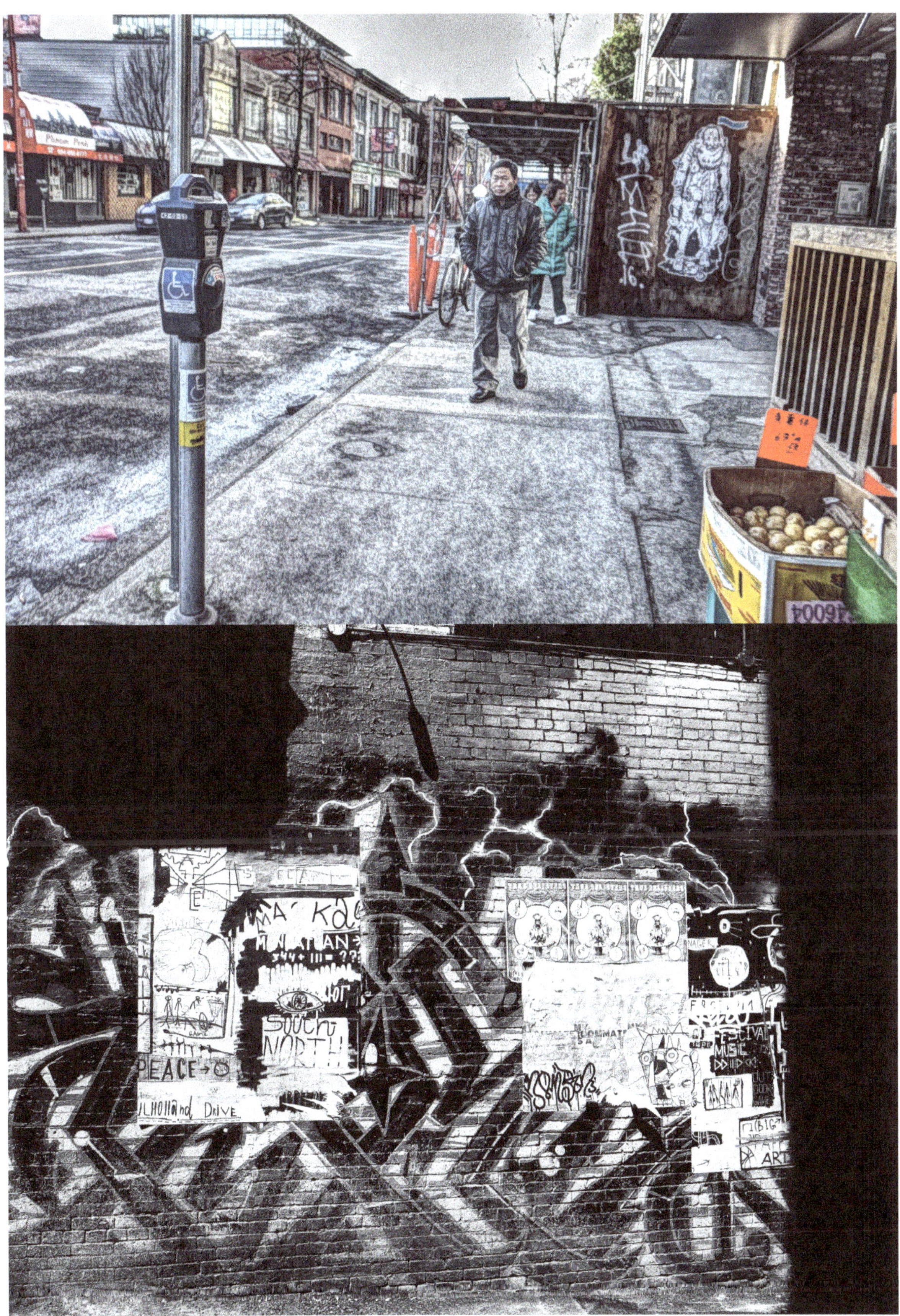

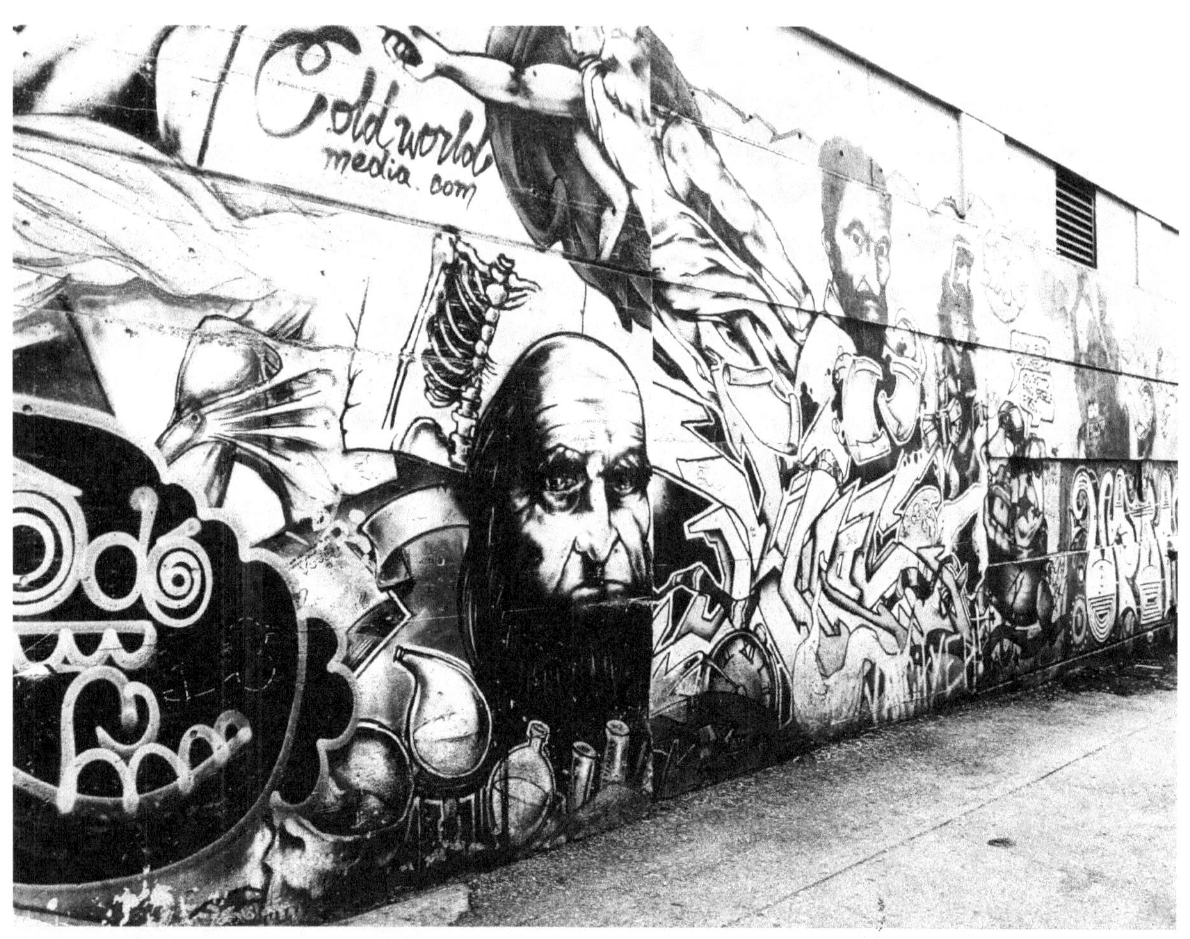
Cold world
media.com

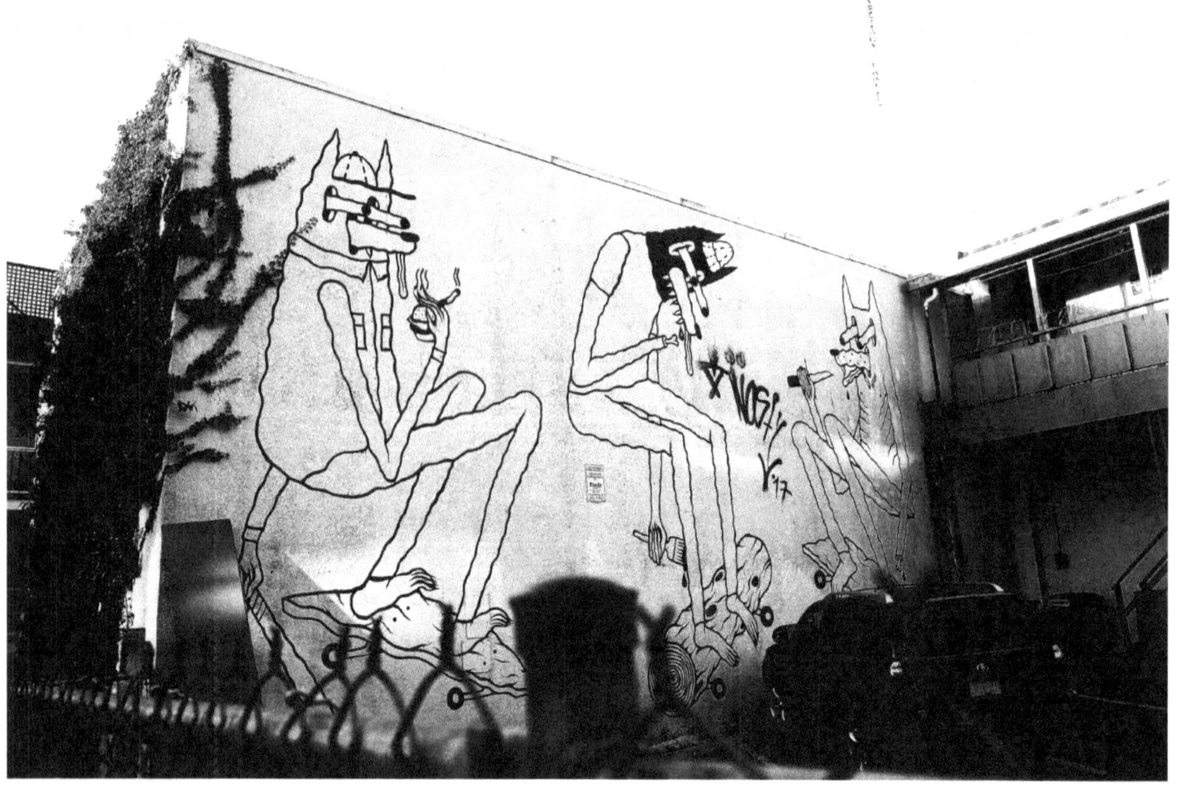

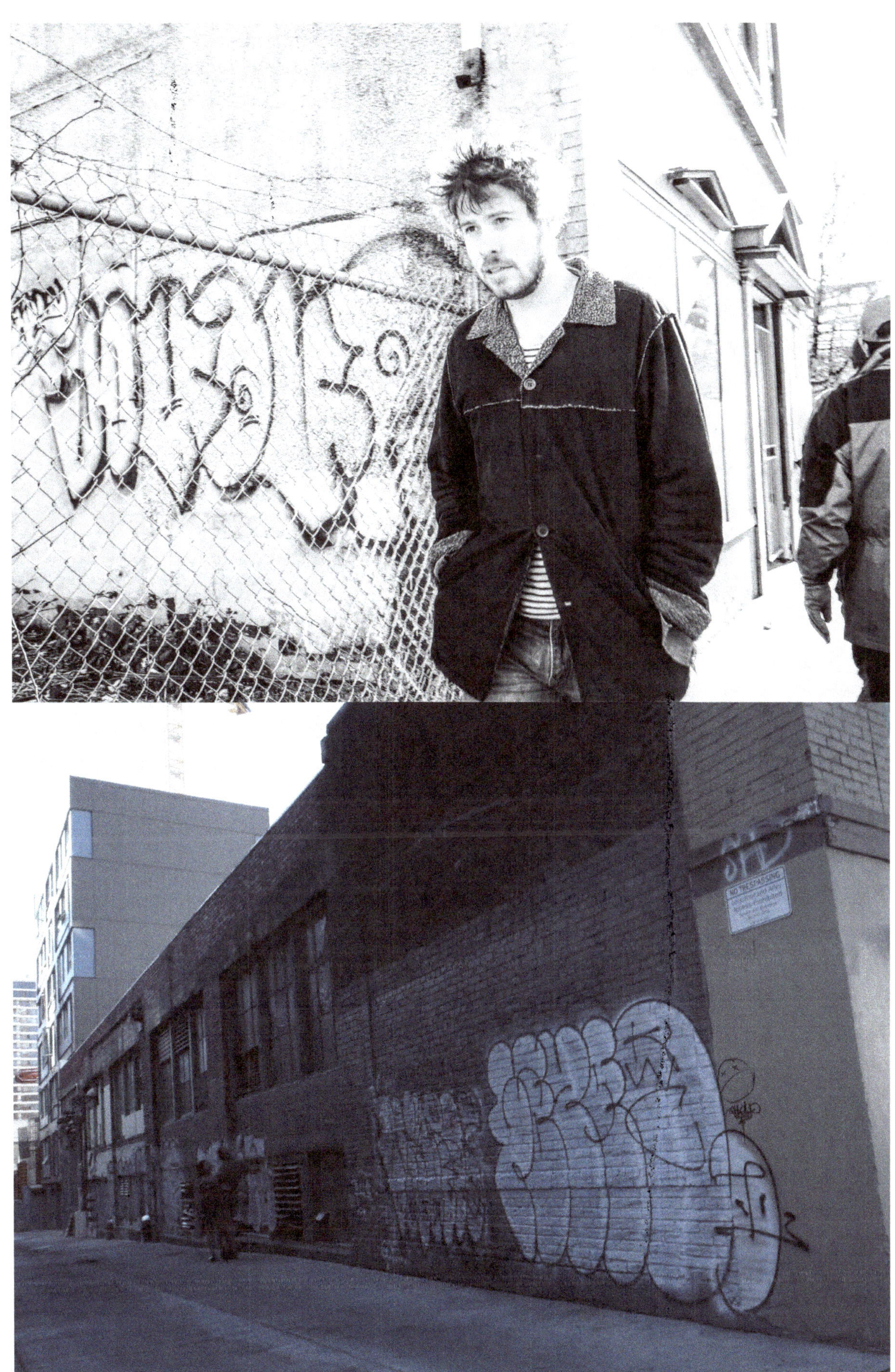

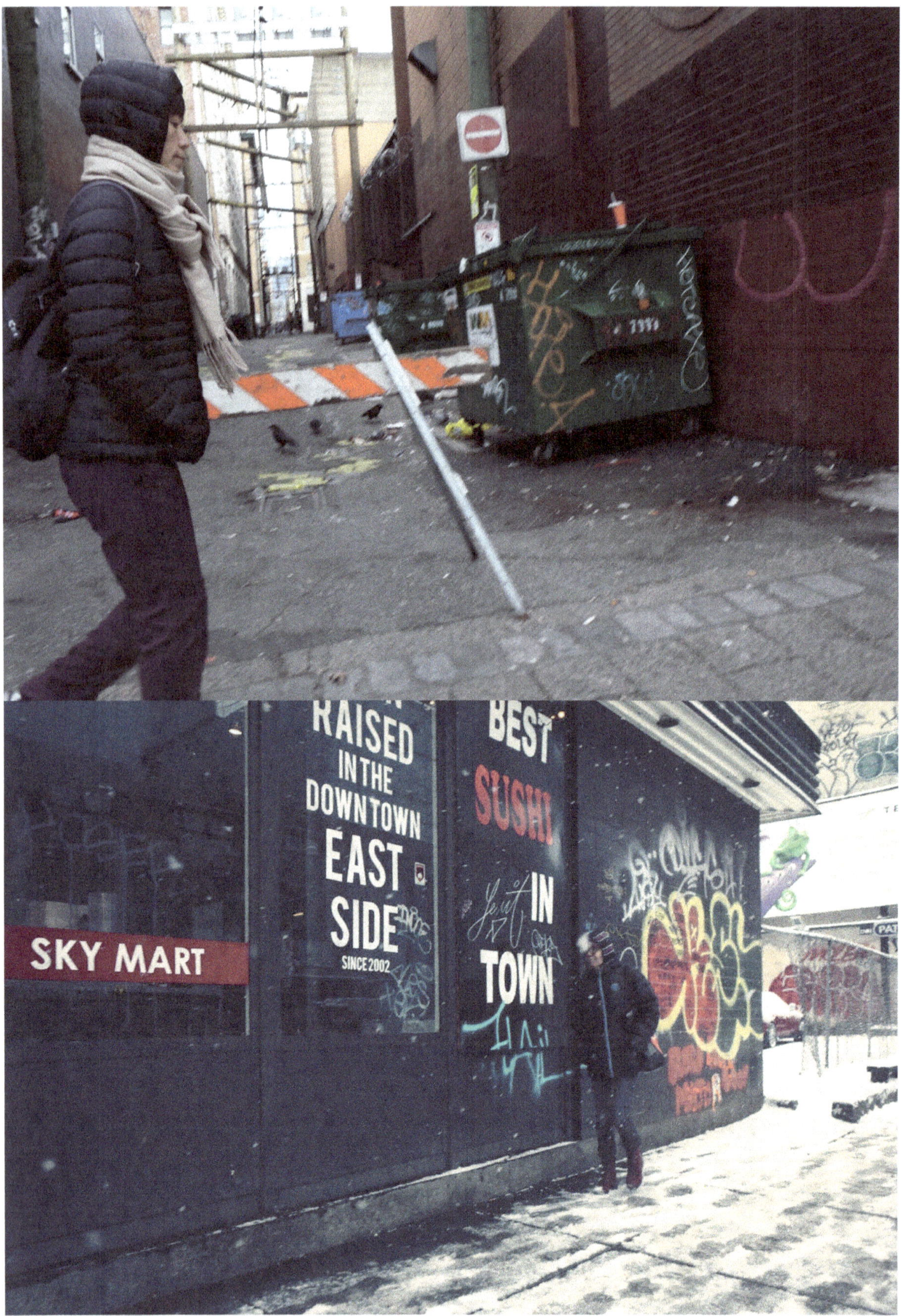
SKY MART
RAISED IN THE DOWNTOWN EAST SIDE
SINCE 2002
BEST SUSHI IN TOWN

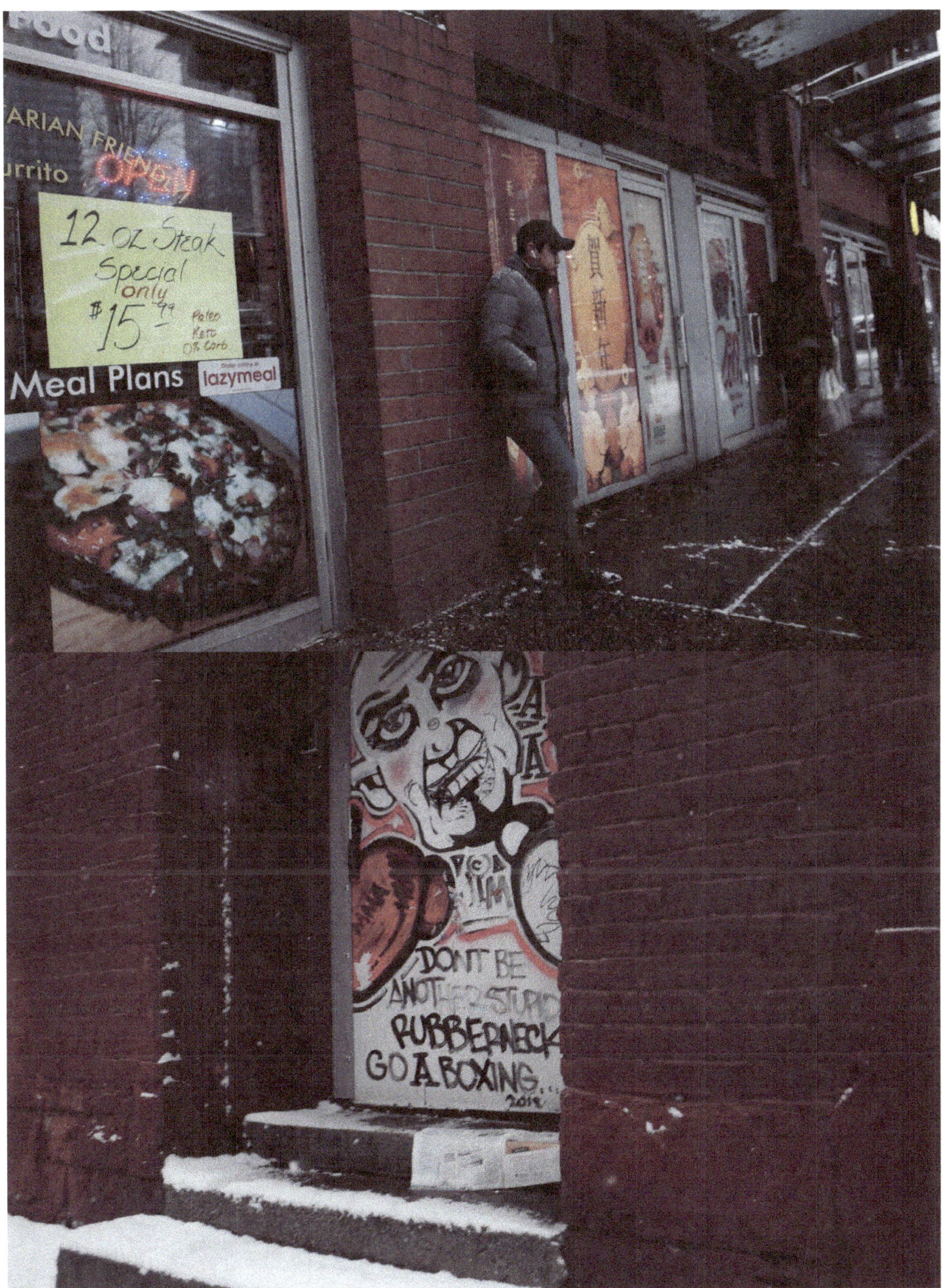
Food
ARIAN FRIENDLY
urrito
OPEN
12 oz Steak
Special
only
$15 99
Paleo
Keto
0% Carb
Meal Plans
lazymeal
DON'T BE
ANOTHER STUPID
RUBBERNECK
GO A BOXING

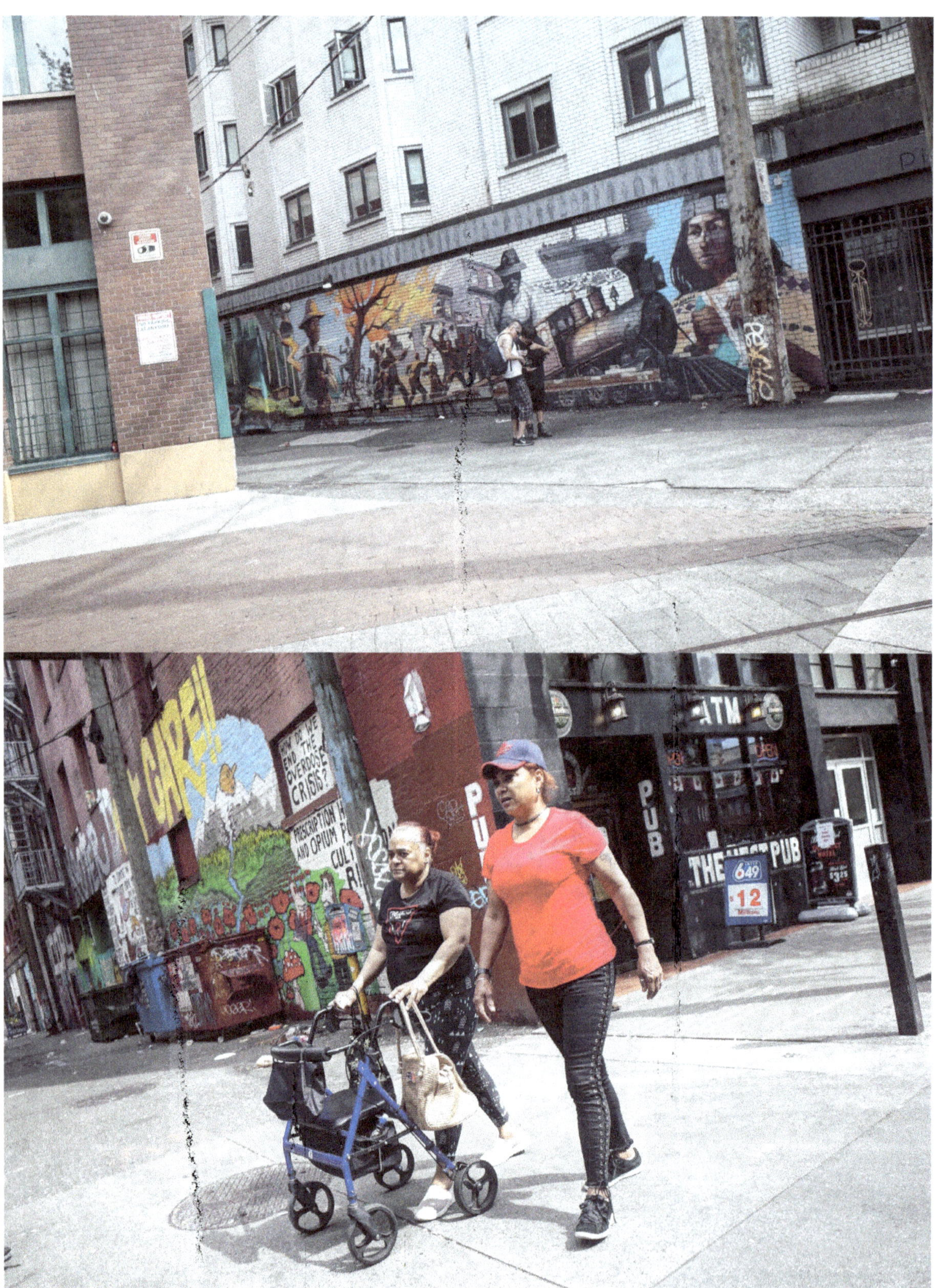
CARE!!
HOW DO WE
END THE
OVERDOSE
CRISIS?
PRESCRIPTION H
AND OPIUM P
CULT
R!
PUB
ATM
THE PUB
6/49
$12
Million

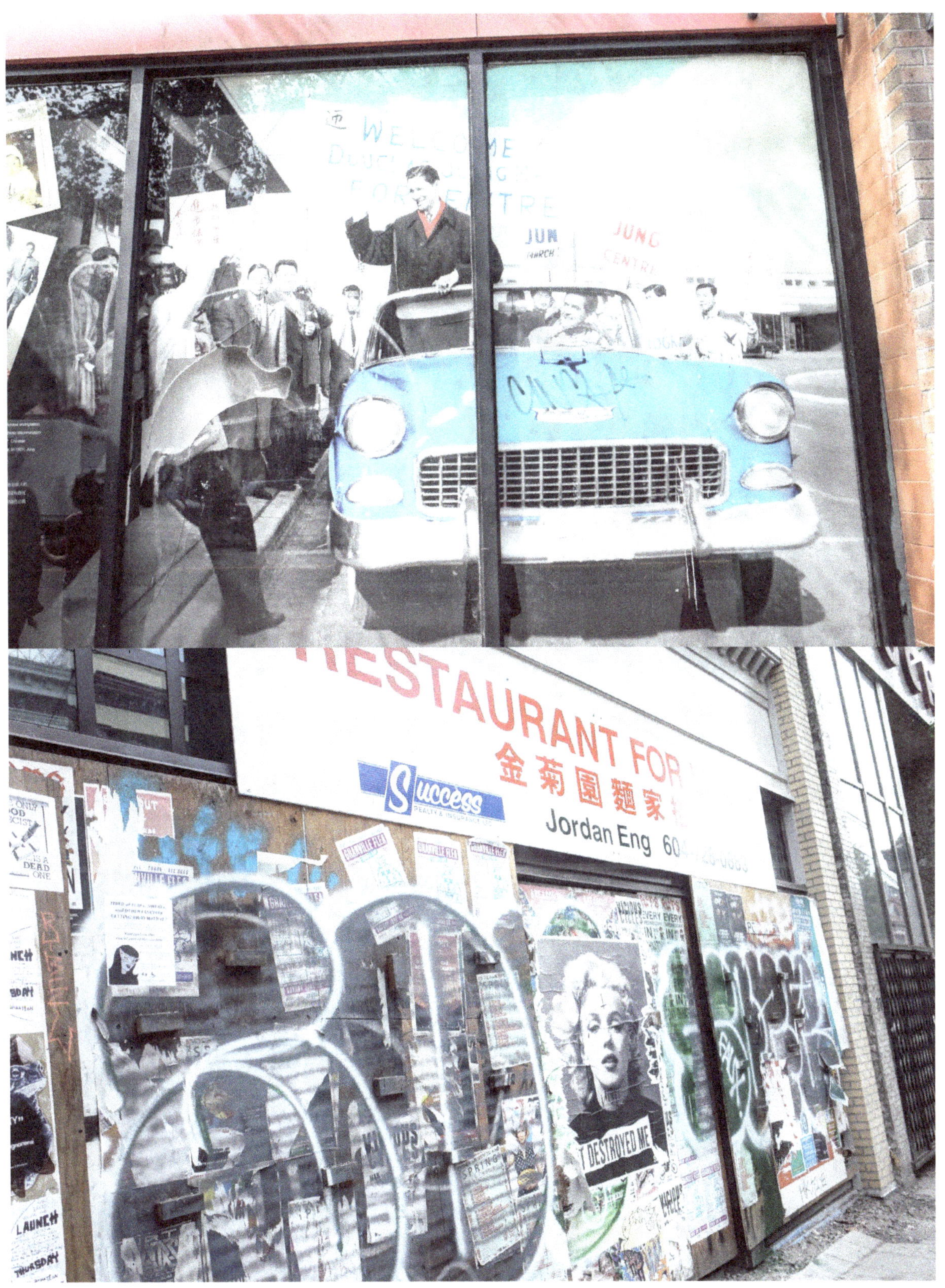
WELCOME
JUN
JUNG
JUN
RESTAURANT FOR
金菊園麵家
Success
REALTY & INSURANCE CO.
Jordan Eng 60
DEAD
ONE
LAUNCH
THURSDAY
T DESTROYED ME

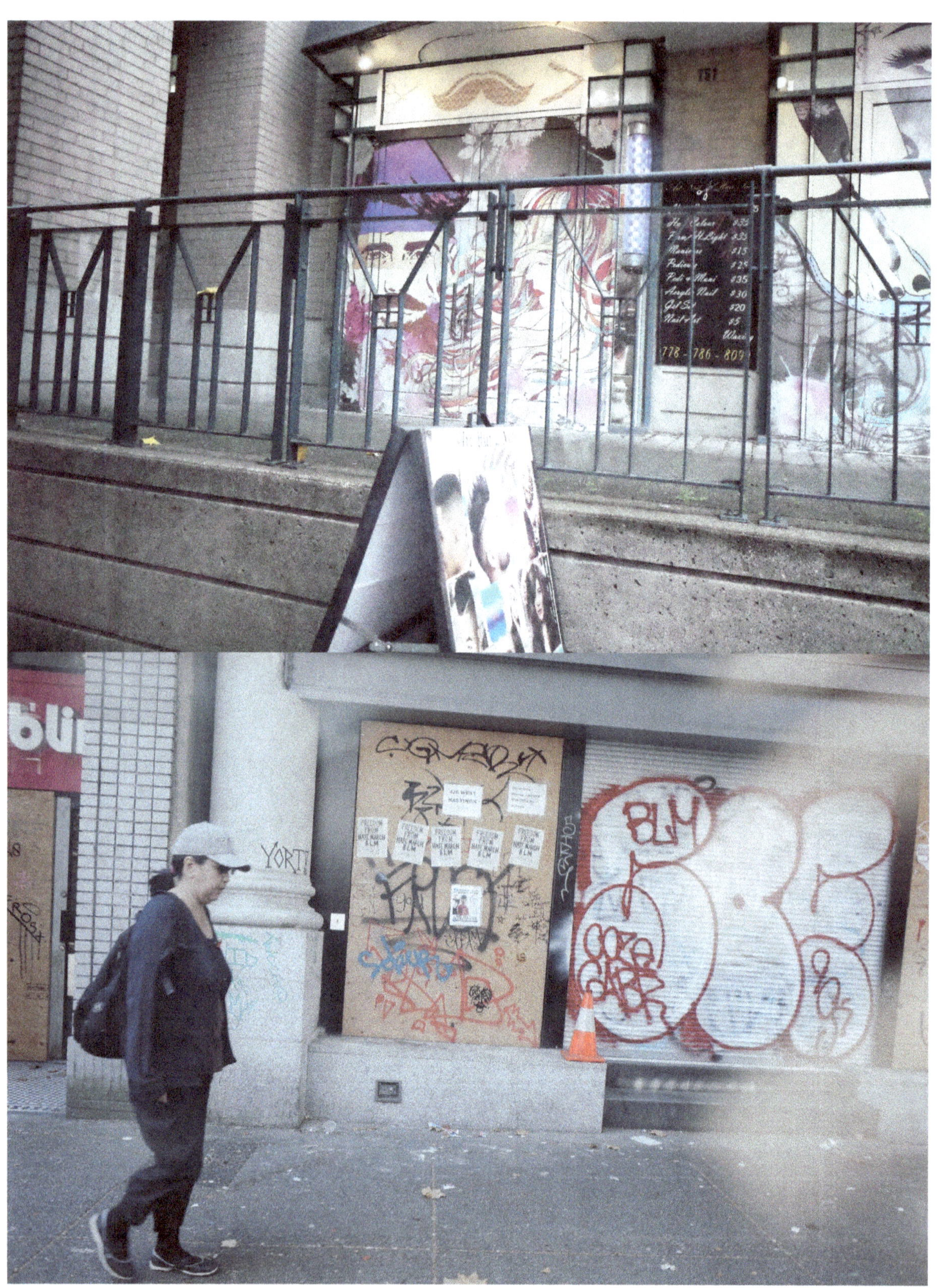

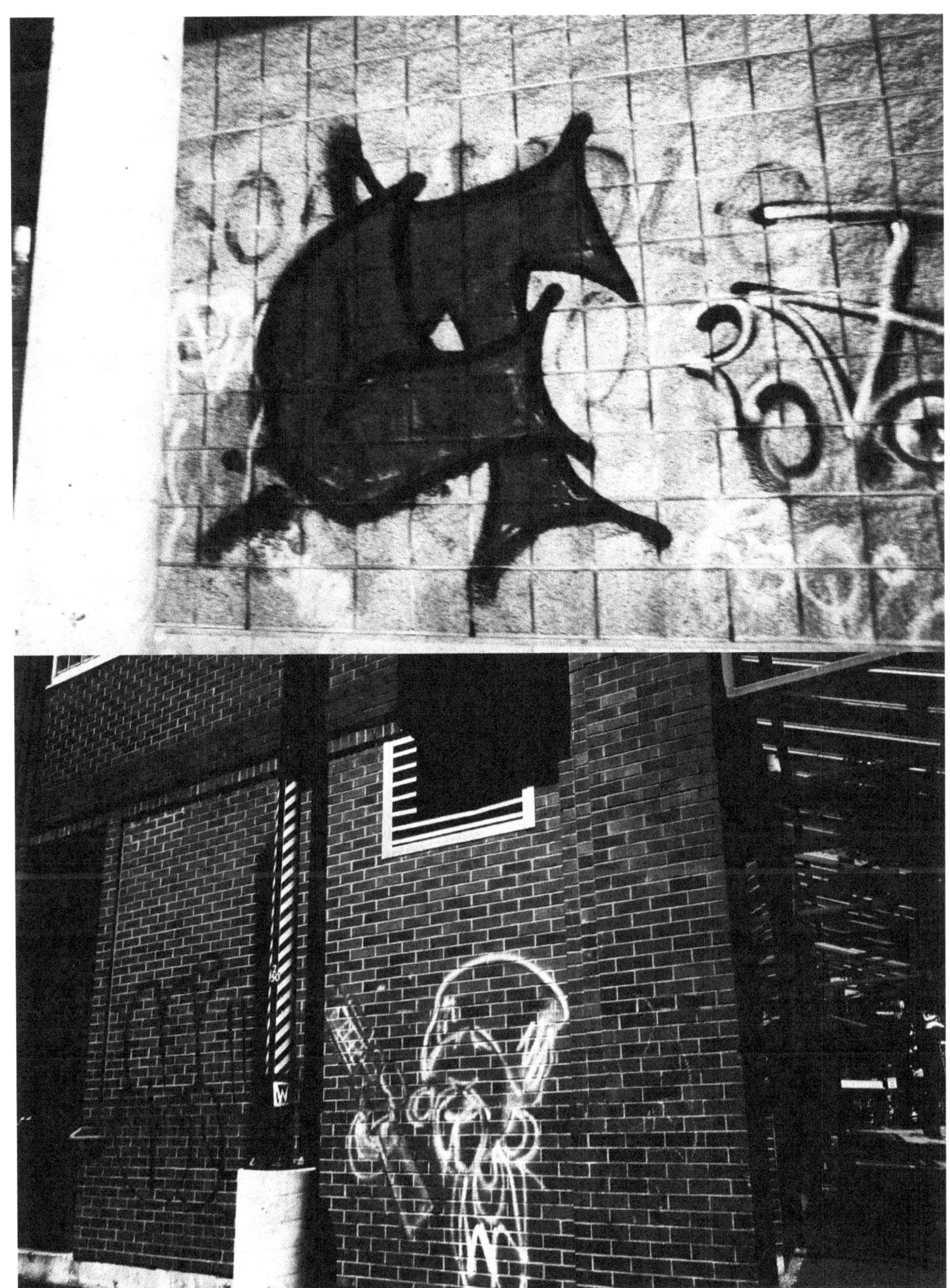

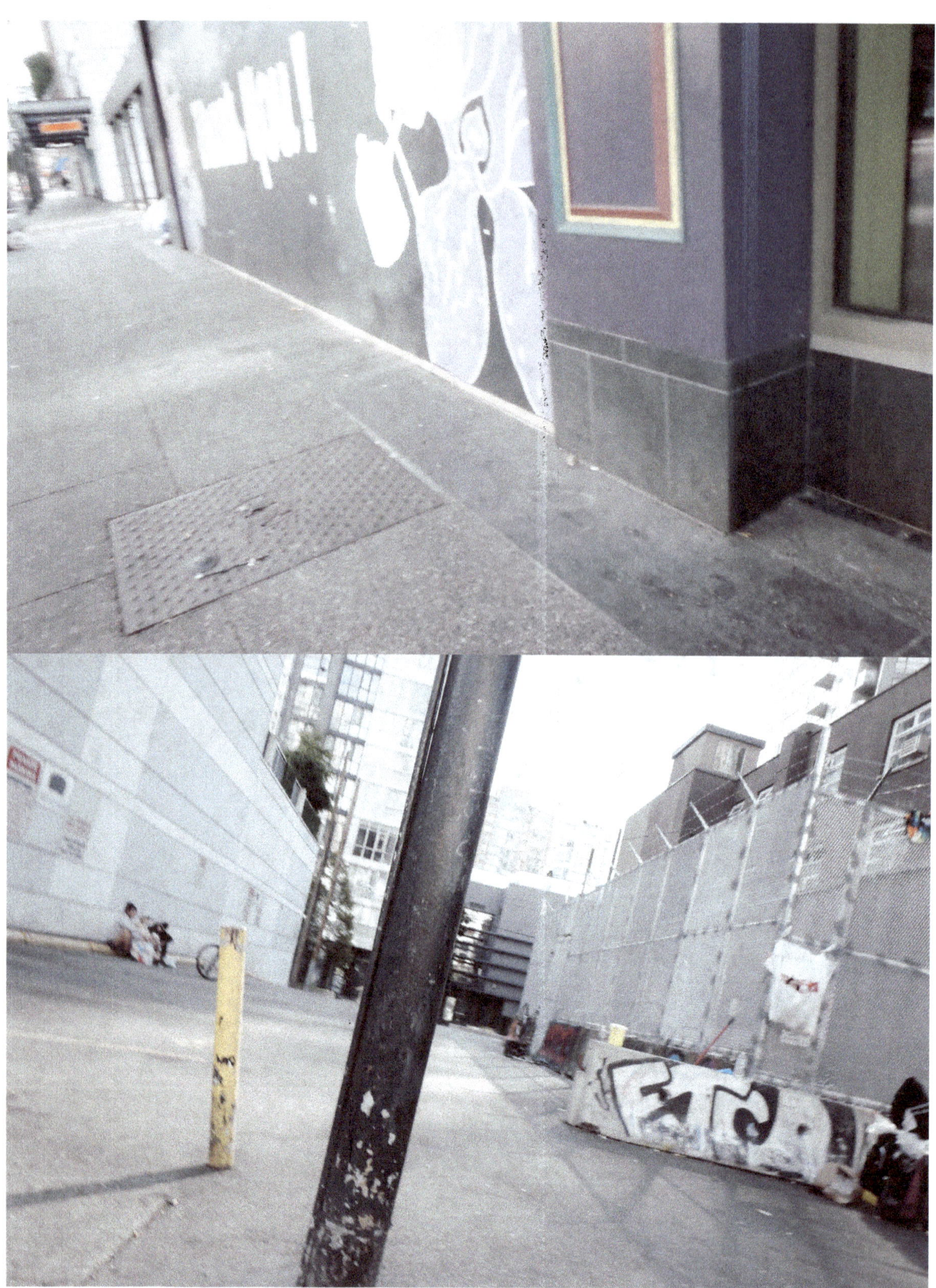

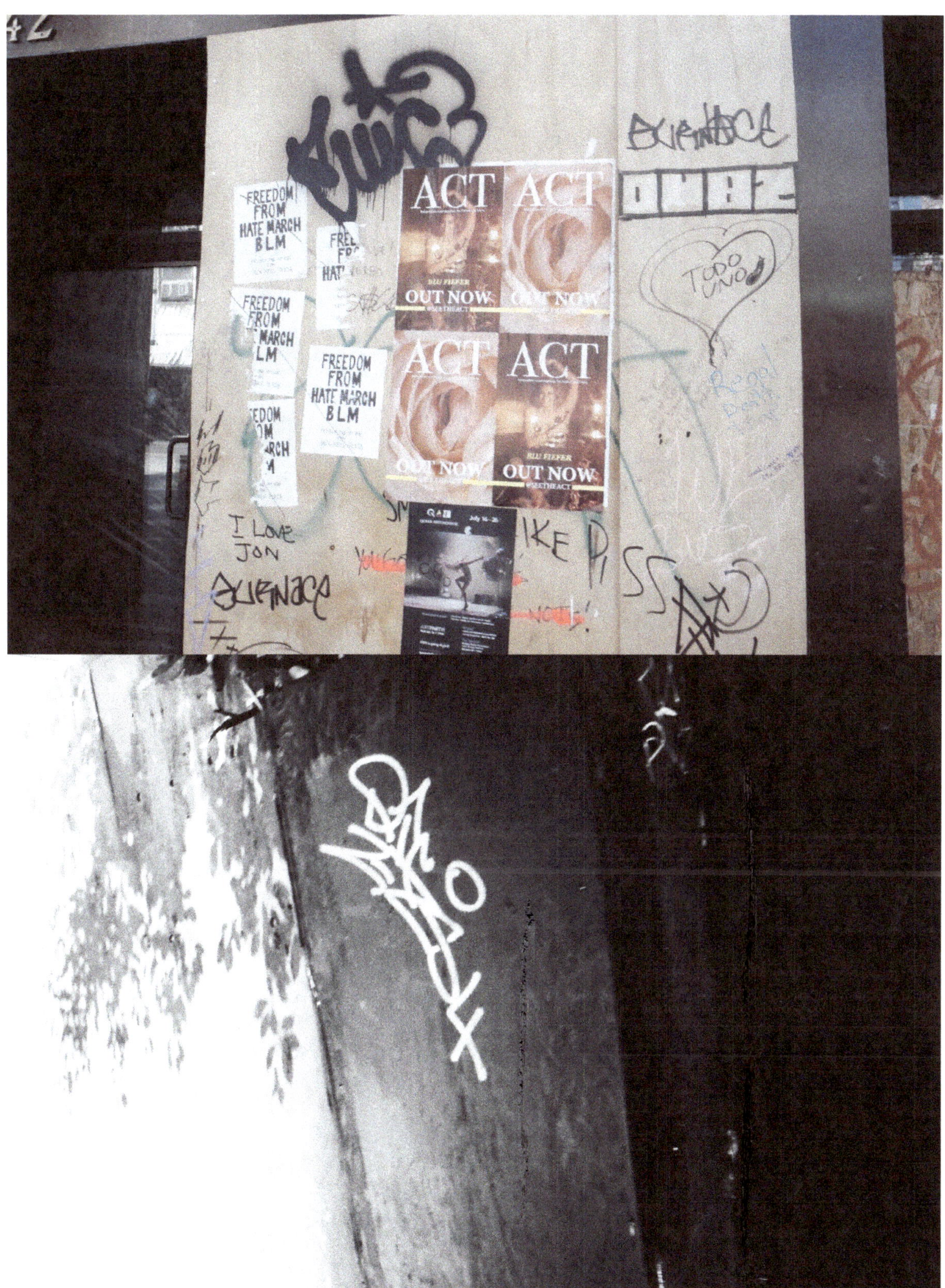
42
SCIENDCE
FREEDOM FROM HATE MARCH BLM
FREEDOM FROM HAT
FREEDOM FROM MARCH LM
FREEDOM FROM HATE MARCH BLM
EDOM OM ARCH
ACT
ACT
BLU FIEFER
OUT NOW
ACT
ACT
BLU FIEFER
OUT NOW
TODO UNO
I LOVE JON
SCIENDCE
IKE PISS
July 14-20

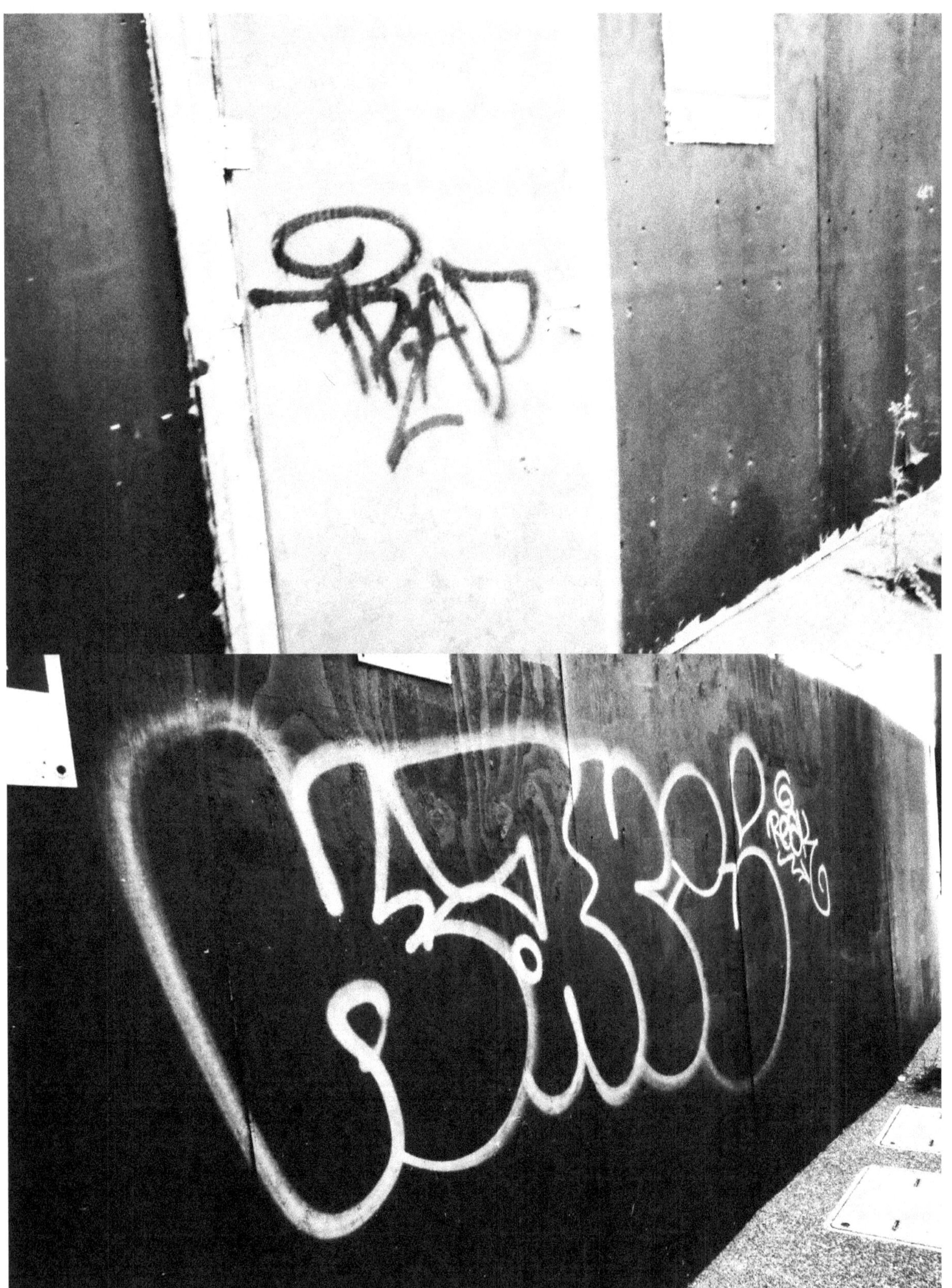

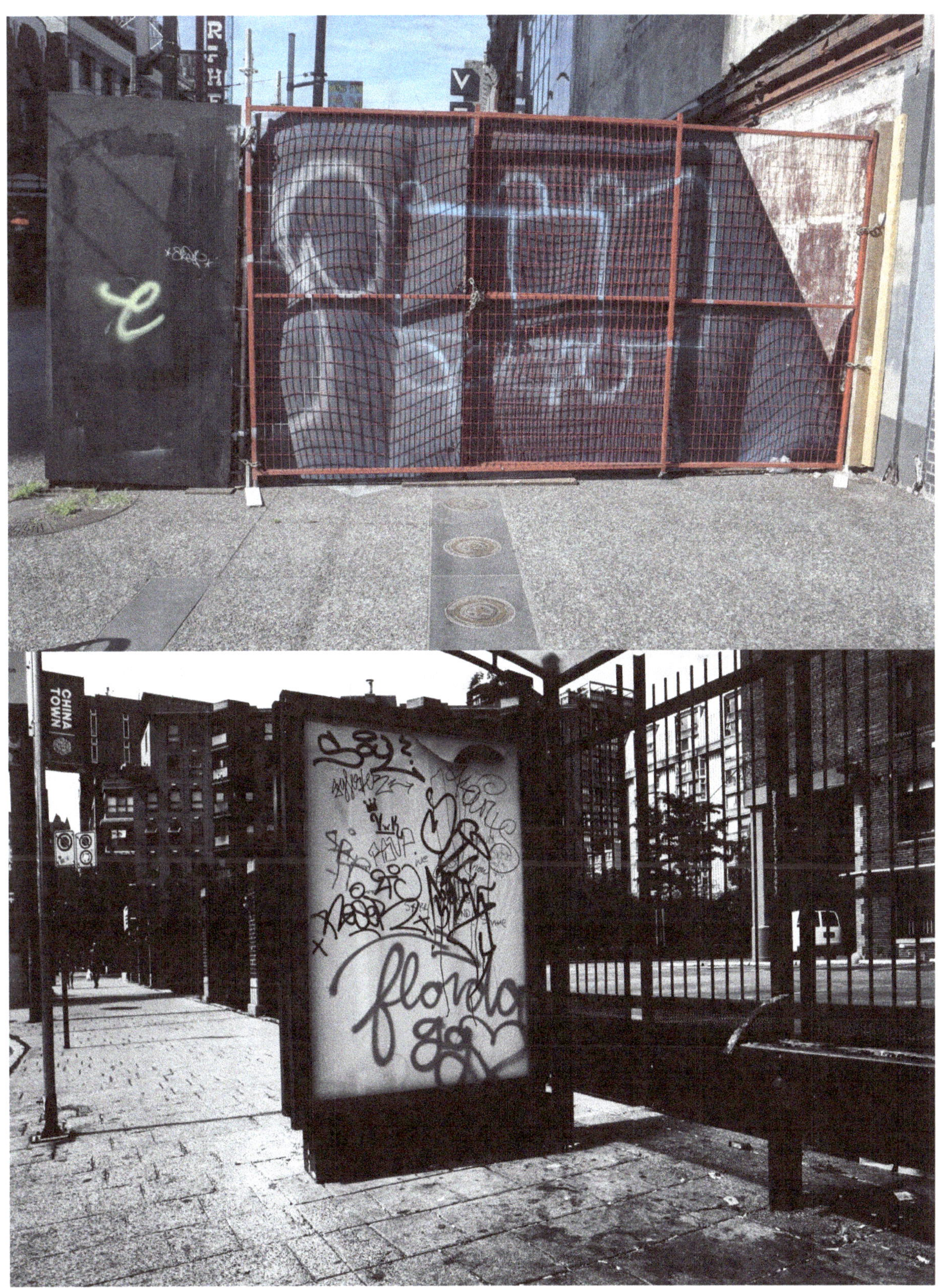
CHINA
TOWN

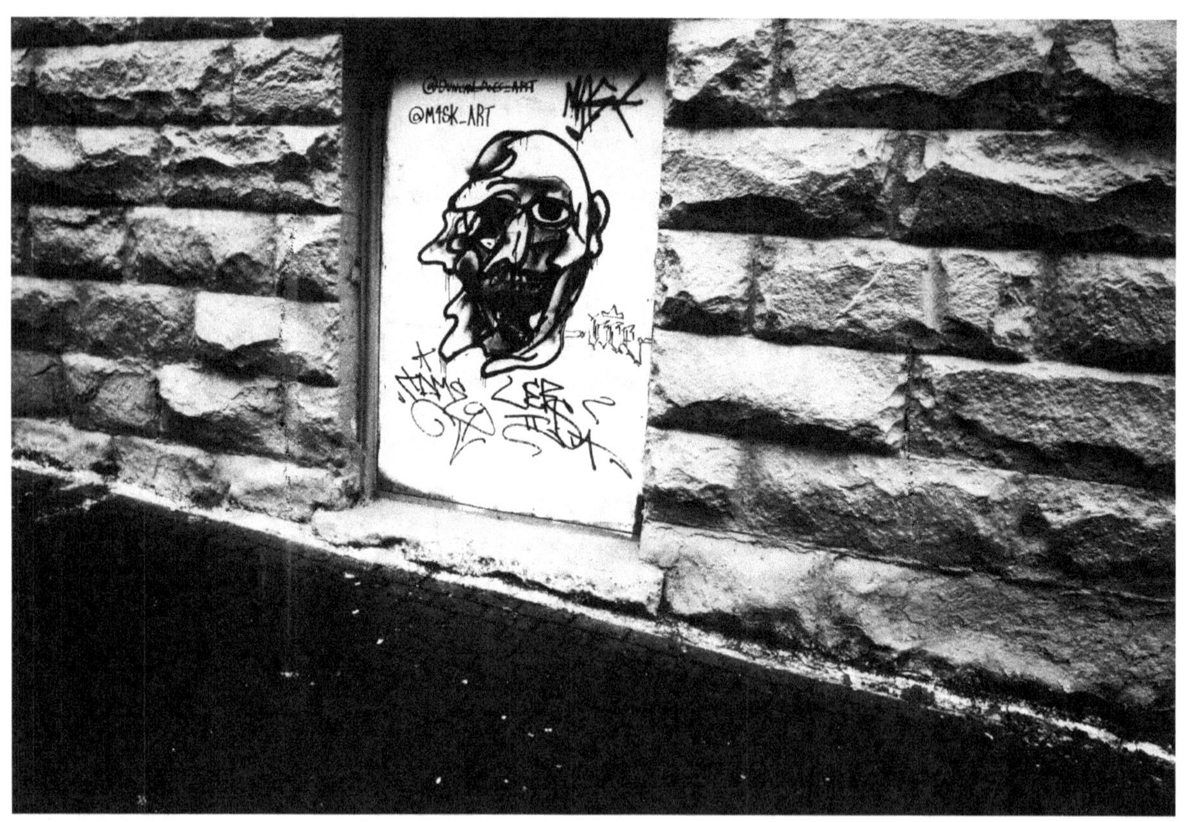

@M1SK_ART

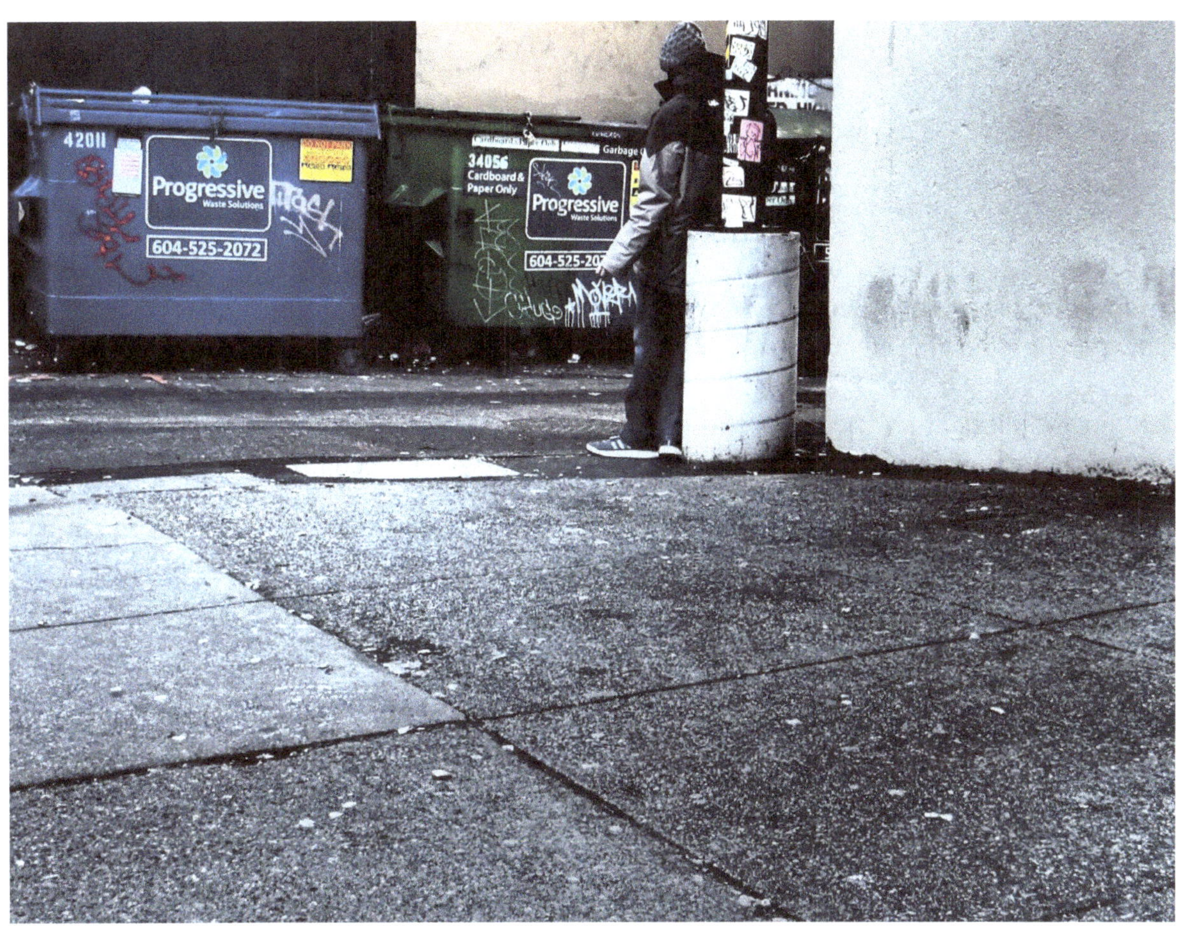
42011
Progressive
Waste Solutions
604-525-2072
34056
Cardboard &
Paper Only
Progressive
Waste Solutions
604-525-20

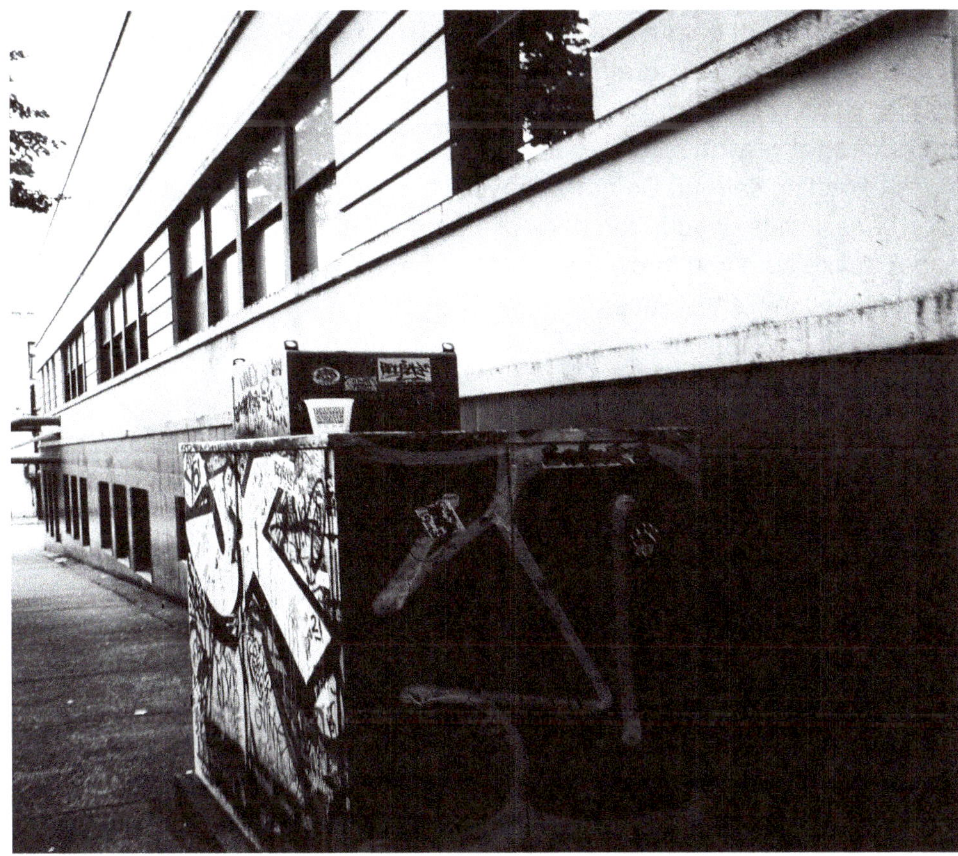

Graffiti Q&A:

1.Where is graffiti alley Vancouver?
Between 5th and 4th Avenue.

2.Is graffiti illegal in Vancouver?
The minimum fine and penalty for anyone doing graffiti without authorization is $500 for each offense under the by-law.

3.How do I report graffiti in Vancouver?
Report online or call VPD non-emergency at 604-717-3321 if your property is vandalized with graffiti.

4.What is the meaning behind the graffiti?
Graffiti, a form of visual communication, is often illegal and involves unauthorized marking in public spaces by individuals or groups. While a common image of graffiti is stylistic symbols or phrases sprayed on walls by street gang members, some graffiti has nothing to do with gangs.

5.What are people who do graffiti called?
One who produces graffiti is known as a: graffitist.

6.How do you not get caught graffiti?
How to reduce the risk of getting caught: Do not write your tags on your personal property, such as schoolbooks, bags, inside of your hat, back of your desk etc. If you want to practice your tag style on paper, make sure you throw the pieces of paper out when you are finished. Keep your sketchbook hidden in a safe place.

7.What do you wear when graffiti?
Like any dress style, there are certain essentials every street artist must have:
Beanie/Hat.
Shirt.
Hoodie.
Watch.
Jeans.
Belt.
Backpack.
Headphone.

8.How do you tell your parents you do graffiti?

if ur under when it comes, tell em how you express yourself. tell them its you expressing yourself, artistically. say it's you getting your art out there, the most efficient way. tell em picasso never sold a painting in his life.

9.Can you go to jail for graffiti?
Adult Penalties.Most graffiti crimes are charged as misdemeanors. City graffiti ordinances typically penalize people convicted of vandalism or graffiti spraying with a fine, though other sentences such as community service, probation and even jail sentences are possible as well.

10.How do graffiti artists make money?
The truth is, a lot of people profit off of Banksy—from dealers who sell his art ripped from the streets to photographers who sell photos of his street art to artists who knock off his style to sell work of their own.

11.Is graffiti artist a job?
In 2018, the average annual salary for fine artists hovered around $48,960. Although graffiti is rapidly gaining acceptance as a true art form, individuals who are interested in pursuing a career in graffiti should be aware that it is still illegal to deface public or private property.

12.How do I become a street artist?
The best way to become a graffiti artist is to develop an original name and a unique style. Start small with sketching, and then start tagging with permanent markers. Develop your skill by meeting other artists and learning the graffiti scene.

13.How much do spray paint artists make?
Street Artist Salary
Annual Salary   Monthly Pay
Top Earners$64,000 $5,333
75th Percentile$45,000 $3,750
Average$41,284 $3,440
25th Percentile$27,000 $2,250

14.How long does it take to learn graffiti?
How long does it take to get good at graffiti? It can take up to 15 years to master the art. After all, it is art, not mess making.

15.What skills do you need to do graffiti?
Beyond artistic talent, a graffiti artist, like all artists, must have a number of abilities and qualities to succeed in such a creative field, which include passion for art and for the graffiti art world specifically, the courage to take risks and grow in the field, an entrepreneurial attitude, focus, willingness to ...

16.How can graffiti be positive?
Not only do street art and graffiti murals improve the general look of a space but the study suggests that it also has the ability to improve the area from a financial aspect which then goes on to benefit the community by creating more jobs within the area, which is especially beneficial for areas were employment ...

17.How much does graffiti art cost?

A low-detail piece that includes one or two colors of traditional graffiti costs about $30 per sq. ft. A medium-detail piece that includes full-color graphics costs about $50 per sq. ft.

18.How do you become a professional spray painter?

The qualifications that you need to work as an industrial spray painter include a high school diploma or GED certificate and the skills to operate spray painting equipment. Many employers train new workers but tend to prefer applicants with at least one year of experience in industrial painting.

19.Why do trains always have graffiti?

Before the sides of freight trains were taken over by urban creatives, railroad workers wrote first graffiti on them, which included "arrival and departure times, weights, and other information about the car's contents for the benefit of their colleagues in distant cities that would be unloading them."

20.Is graffiti good for cities?

Cities that have more graffiti tend to be cultural and artistic hubs. And street art tends to give people who don't have the resources to launch a more traditional art career a shot.

21.Why is graffiti so important?

Graffiti and street art embody cultural significance through its individualistic nature, though its ability to beautify and enhance public spaces, and 1 Page 12 through its highly visible way of speaking out on political, social and economic issues, because it so clearly represents an artistic subculture with a message ...

22.Is graffiti harmful to society?

Graffiti can cause damage to decorative or delicate surfaces. Affected areas may also start to feel run down and appear threatening, putting off customers and prospects. Some graffiti can be very offensive, threatening to groups or individuals, or racially abusive.

23.How long does graffiti paint last?

I have been a professional graffiti artist for 30 years and only use the best quality spray paint products available. I guarantee the quality of my materials from peeling or flaking for 1-year. Many of my outdoor works last 5-8 years in the outdoor elements.

24.What do graffiti artists use?

Spray paint is the most popular type of paint graffiti artists use because it's portable, extremely versatile and easy to get hold of. Ever since modern-day graffiti's early beginnings in the 1960s, spray paint has been the most popular medium for graffiti.

25.Why do graffiti artists tag?

...of graffiti, known as "tagging," which entailed the repeated use of a single symbol or series of symbols to mark territory. In order to attract the most attention possible, this type of graffiti usually appeared in strategically or centrally located neighborhoods.

26.Who spray paints trains?

Check out our list of 5 train masters whose work you have to see to believe.
Jaber, aka The White Ninja aka Freight King.
Revok From Walls to Freights to Everything In Between.
Troy Lovegates, aka Other aka Freight Master.
Freight Graffiti Master - MECRO.
ESKAE - Freight Graffiti.

27.When did train graffiti start?
Railroad graffiti began in earnest during the 1920s and especially the Depression years of the 1930s, as hobos and even some railroad workers made chalk drawings on freight cars to mark their presence. That practice continues in the 21st century; drawings made by "Colossus of Roads" are among the most popular.

28.What are the 3 major types of graffiti?
Types of graffiti.
Tag. Tagging is the easiest and simplest style of graffiti; it includes one color and the artist's name or identifier. ...
Throw-up or a bomb. Sometimes called a "throwie" is a simple form of graffiti, sitting between a tag and a bomb. ...
Letters. Letters can be different styles. ...
Piece or character.

29.Do spray cans expire?
We guarantee a shelf life of 10 years after production for our cans, with the exception of Granite Effect which has a shelf life of 5 years, if appropriate storage is provided. The storage temperature should be between 10°-25°C (50°-77°F) and the relative air humidity should not exceed 60%.

30.Is spray paint permanent?
You get the best of both worlds. Once sprayed, all the water in the paint evaporates quickly, leaving a flexible acrylic film of color behind. The color is permanent and doesn't move - which means you can over-paint without bleeding and achieve multi-layered surface effects.

31.Is there a graffiti language?
Modern graffiti is a language largely developed in urban centers like New York City, starting in the 1970s. During that time, funding for arts education in public schools was down. Kids started tagging walls and subway cars as a form of self expression. "Media called it graffiti, but we called it writing.

32.Why do trains allow graffiti?
Before the sides of freight trains were taken over by urban creatives, railroad workers wrote first graffiti on them, which included "arrival and departure times, weights, and other information about the car's contents for the benefit of their colleagues in distant cities that would be unloading them."

33.Why is there so much graffiti on trains?
In order to avoid what was almost becoming persecution in some neighborhoods, and for their artwork to be maintained for longer – as well as being able to see it travel across the

United States – many graffiti artists turned to freight trains and left the subway, and the streets, behind.

34.Can you use a hairdryer to dry spray paint?
Blowing dry, COOL air that helps carry the evaporating solvent away from the paint is fine, but you risk blowing dust onto the surface.

35.Is graffiti considered art or vandalism?
Graffiti is seen as a form of artistic expression and can have positive outcomes for people, it is also illegal and considered vandalism.

36.Is graffiti an art lesson?
Graffiti-inspired study can build fundamental art skills and knowledge while authentically motivating every student. Structuring a graffiti unit can be a challenge, especially in the early weeks.

37.Who made graffiti famous?
Cornbread. Born Darryl McCray, Cornbread is generally acknowledged to be the first modern graffiti artist, who got his start tagging in Philadelphia during the late 1960s.

38.Why is my spray paint soft?
Softness. This happens when your paint is soft after it is dry, making it susceptible to water spotting and fingerprints for days after your paint job. This happens **when you spray the undercoat or topcoat too heavily or don't give sufficient drying time between the coats**.

39.Is my child a tagger?
Some indications that your child may be a tagger are: a. Your child stays out until early morning or all night. b. Your child frequently wears a large backpack or baggy pants.

40.How do you stop graffiti?
5 Strategies for Graffiti and Vandalism Prevention:1.Anti-Graffiti Film. One of the most cost-effective ways to prevent graffiti and vandalism damage is anti-graffiti film. 2.Impact Protection Attachment Systems. 3.Anti-Graffiti Paints and Coatings. 4.Barriers. 5.Multi-Layer Surface Protection Film.

41.Can graffiti be viewed as art?
The idea that a form of artistic expression could be considered vandalism is, unsurprisingly, not widespread among graffiti artists. "Graffiti is 100% art," says Pearce. "It's a symbol of rebellion, and it presents a fantastic new form of creativity, but what makes it art is an individual's opinion.

42.What materials are graffiti proof?

HDPE (high-density polyethylene) is a solid plastic that can stand up to graffiti. Due to its homogenous coloring, it doesn't absorb the paint, and any graffiti can simply be wiped away without having to paint over it.

43.Why does graffiti affect our community?

Loss of sense of community.It's known that the appearance of graffiti often encourages further crime. Young adults and teenagers are easily influenced, and are therefore most at risk of turning to vandalism. To prevent youth crime, education is key.

44.What is mottling in paint?

What is mottling or streaking? This is when the metallic particles in a refinishing material "float" together and can form a streaking pattern or "tiger stripes". One of the common causes of mottling is a spray gun being held too close to the surface causing the refinishing material to be applied too wet.

www.ingramcontent.com/pod-product-compliance
Lightning Source LLC
Chambersburg PA
CBHW080844160726
47999CB00009B/3005